AF230502

EDITOR-IN-CHIEF
Eileen Cleary

ASSISTANT EDITOR
Elizabeth Mercurio

ASSOCIATE EDITOR
Christine Jones

FLASH FICTION EDITORS
Mark Jednaszewski   Sarah Walker

ART EDITOR
Lisa Sullivan

BOOK REVIEW EDITOR
Amanda Shaw

VISPO EDITOR
Suzanne Mercury

WEB EDITOR
Rebecca Connors

MEDIA AND EVENTS
Frances Donovan

READERS
Susan Kay Anderson, Jules Jacob,
K. T. Landon, Michelle Lynch, Gloria Monaghan, Catherine Morocco,
Tzynya Pinchback, Sarah Dickenson Snyder, Mark Walsh,
Anastasia Vassos, Art Zilleruelo

COVER ART, ISSUE 9
Painting by Kathleen Frank, "From the Loneliest Road"

© 2023. All rights reserved. This material may not be published, or reprinted
without the express consent of the authors or artists attributed here.

ASKOLD MELNYCZUK

Melancholy Baby

Go:
Join the March
wind flicking the nude
oak: enter
the leeched minarets
of the grass, the soaked
sigh of stunned
flesh slowly
turning, as after
love, while
the adulterous starlings
sing down the sun
off-key adieus, and the last
snow lingers like
the memory of promise
stayed by the breath of others,
though your own hands reached out
to trace a lineage once felt accessible
as air, drawn from the wind, from a world
where Walden seasoned the Ganges, and wheat
battened on blood—pull back
from this new season
sheltering always
and ever more beautiful
lusts, the same
still, from all
you've seen, touched, dreamed, remembering
"who maketh the darkness his convert...."
What's sightless eyes us best
and from the syllables of things
we're made a living speech
to testify we're seen.
Admit to the stones they know
more than you, and are you.

ASKOLD MELNYCZUK

Sweet Enough

Astor Piazzola
rakes the accordion, scoring
the other side

of tango,
it is that sweet
and hides a whip in it;

the cat stalks
summer in the window,
dynamite in the trees;

you leave again
for the south;
I worry;

when
this Christ air
shivers the room.

I lie still
under the lights
under the ceiling fan:

but to be
a disciple
is another thing—

like music
becoming applause.
And I have known

that sensation
sweet enough
to kill time

I'll call Christ,
it is that light:
like, who

ever wanted to
hurt anyone, who
asked for it?

Not Tonita,
of Salvador,
hurrying home

after bringing lunch
to her husband to nurse
her baby but the baby

with its brothers,
beg pardon, not them,
their torsos, were already sitting

around the table,
heads on platters,
hands stroking

their skulls.
Where was the Jesus
feeling for her?

Can't say.
All I can:
a strange light

some people give off, from
and within
the heart, ceilings

lift, the *pajaros*
fly in, and the cat
in Christ himself

stirs awake, blinking
interest. For Tonita
this day was second

nature, she had already
dreamed it, lived
her whole

life in grace
always knowing,
always sure

she owned nothing
but what the heart
could save in its fist:

so should we thank
our money
or helping this?

This not prosaic event.
This pure poetry
in our time? To write

love, is to remember,
is more. And not.
To write is to leave

Christ and Tonita
and you
entering the hieratic

privacies of the spirit
not easily named
or forgiven.

4

ASKOLD MELNYCZUK

My Life Against the Berlin Wall

Martin, Thomas touched
the wound
like *colibri* beebalm:
better not to fly through glass!

And Abraham gave Isaac,
a story
I've never fully understood,
which makes it good,
and worth repeating.

The ties, invisible
silk cords binding us
to this earth
Able needed to escape from
are thinner than ever today.

And the Bible
stories oddly near
as I walk, encouraging
squirrels not to fall:
pray keep your balance!

on this Indian
Summer November Tuesday.
I wonder if they know
these days, being beautiful,
won't last, and will

give way again
to the bureaucracies of ice
and protocols of snow.
But the myth
of the blue sky

seems more
than tale,
though you can't
touch it, package it, or keep it
going after dark

while what we know
of freedom hovers
bright under its tender
sway, the sweet
percussive nothingness

of faith. The frontier
of being is nothing
less than the next
breath, and yet
this listless eye

can't help not seeing
that the front's
not here, but further south,
because the skin
which breathes above the skin

like an expansive fog, flowing
outward, south and east, and even
west, where they believe
they know the score, the skin
prickles and the sick

spirit sobs, feeling cut.
And so, maybe
I need to see
just when
slicing through the carrot to

my thumb, I can't
keep from fingering
the flap of flesh,
so loose and tentative and there.
Faith it was

walked up
and touched
a living God;
from then on knew
just what to do.

ASKOLD MELNYCZUK

A Potato Reading Rilke

Suddenly the crap has meaning:
old wallets, scarves, the radio
years in a drawer, batteries, blue
shirt, the almost new
sweaters, the scarred belts.

Apocatastasis of objects!
Someone else will one day squirm
inside the suit from Syms
your father bought you
for some funeral, or wedding.

To this day you've been
a potato reading Rilke,
skipping every other word
to get the moral at the end,
a morsel of meaning

you could mouth
like a seduction song your spirit
needed, lost inside
the jazz of lights, the stop
and go, with clouds hallucinating

rain and dirt the poor,
a key to how to walk
into a bookstore or a bar.
The walls heard you all
too often, the air

aged with you.
Still the centripetal flower,
the secret presence
planted in the heart
of our life's decay

argues with Trotsky who
like all prophets, loved
the future tense too much:
this is not lies.
Matter dreaming finds

a sweetness light permits
its sickest kids.
And he: Yeah, sure.
But the junk in your closet
rises like Lazarus because

they, on this planet, have needs
you can answer.
Pack your suitcase, green
nylon from Spain, pack it
full of that

manufactured ego,
and go.

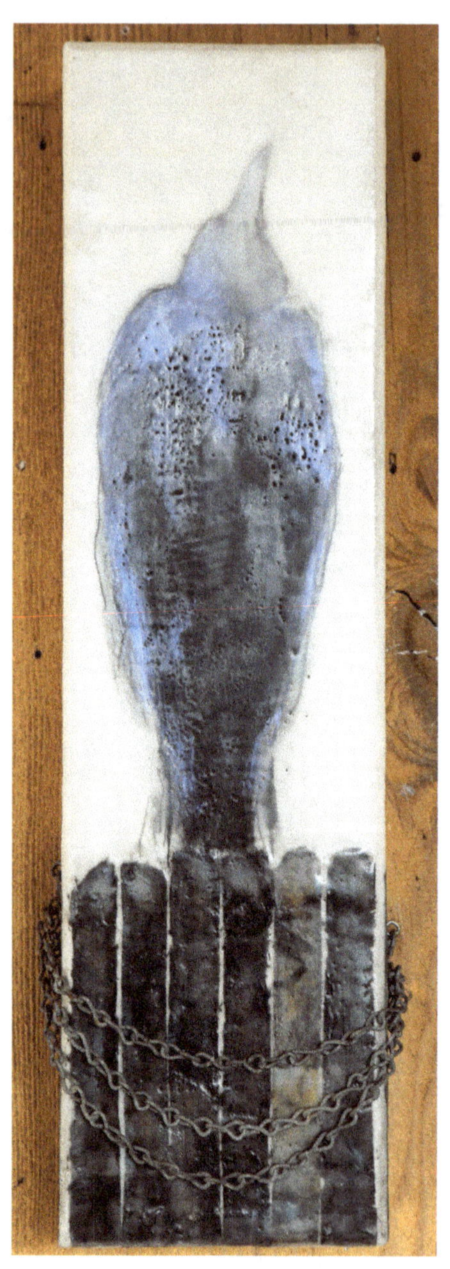

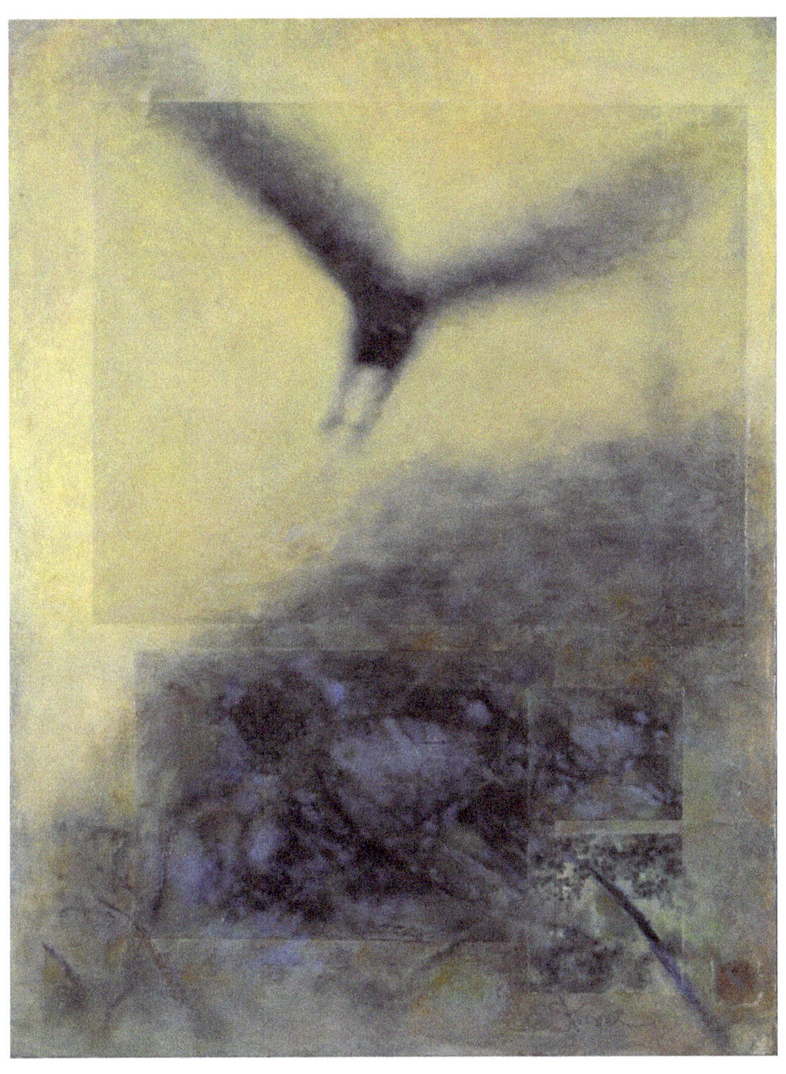

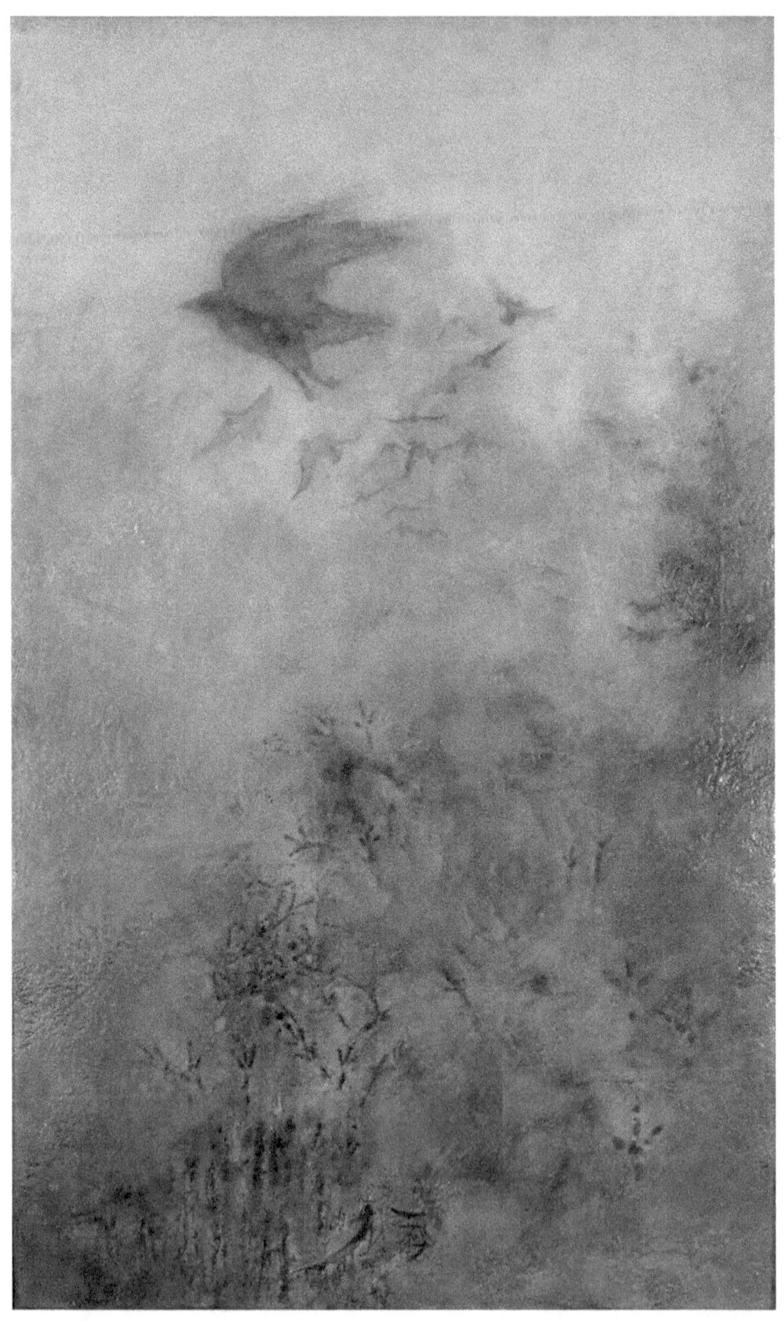

MICHAEL JONES

After Practicing Bach's Chaconne

"... the man writes a whole world ..."   – *Brahms*

I cradle my violin, as if
unwritten notes, sounded on shells,
were not re-crossing the oceans.
Then I abandon that pose, recalling
the maker's story – how in Bosnia
he found this maple, the best, surrounded
with trees that had been fretted by gunfire.
How the wind was playing through those.

LAURE-ANNE BOSSELAAR

Kite at Daybreak on the Cliff's Edge

At first, I think it's a plastic bag, ripped to ribbons
& billowing wild inside a wild wind. But when it
drops toward the beach I see the man, ancient,
ragged. He pulls a spool to his heart, turns, faces
the cliff & unwinds the string to let his kite rise
up again, but toward me this time. It sways,
soars high into the light-soaked sky as the day
opens to the sun. But the winds shift & lift
the kite higher & toward the ocean. The man
tugs at the spool, pulls back hard, rewinds
the string. The kite resists, pulls, pulls madly
toward the horizon, but the string will not break —
so it lets go, falls slowly toward the sands and lies
down, terribly still, at the feet of its maker.

TOM VERSTEEG

At Cascade Head

who smashed up all this
light and just left it lying here
on the face of the deep
if I could tell I would
bow down to that vandal
with my whole heart and begin
to cry out in thanks

K.T. LANDON

I Will Remember for Both of Us

Butterfly glioma sounds almost pretty,
but it means inoperable, and the present
slipping away from you as quickly as it arrives.
So we leaf though the old albums, the past
all that's left.

    Toddlers together in sailor dresses.

        The high school cast photos from *Hello, Dolly!*,
        me the lead, you in the chorus.

    Two little girls in our grandparents' back yard,
    matching yellow dresses, white anklets, white
    patent Mary Janes, fabulous plastic sunglasses.

You being crowned Miss Summer Scamper
at the Y's day camp, me standing behind,
runner-up for a change.

    Thirteen annual father-daughter nights,
    featuring every fashion faux pax of the seventies
    in garish polyester progression.

        The cake in the shape of a piano
        that you made for my birthday
        the summer you took a decorating class
        when you were going to be a historian
        and I was going to be a musician.

We laugh, and I rest my head
on your shoulder, just to feel you there.

At the terminal in Denver, you cry.
"You're leaving and I'll forget you
were ever here." I kiss you goodbye,
for not yet the last time.

K.T. LANDON

Honeybee at Dusk

In the fading flowers,
like an old woman fumbling

for some forgotten keepsake,
plumbing each golden bloom

for its last sweetness, heedless
until the October cold

pins her to the ground,
far from the hive with its safety,

its thousands of humming
bodies, their warmth and their need.

Or is she waiting until the last
moment, alive to the risk, but lost in—

is it pleasure or duty, so late,
and with darkness coming on?

GLORIA MINDOCK

Crows

The Crows are perched on the
back fence, warning me of death
Graceful in their waiting like my
mother and her mother before her

After death, the birds bring gifts
to help with mourning, when life is gone
The crows know that everything ends
up in the abyss

Guarding the transition, the abandoning
of earth, through all the grief,
memories scatter in the grass as I
walk and they chatter

Give me my brothers back, my mom—
to live an infinite life among us
Images returning before they disappear
once more
A crossroad where we all connect
feeling the same air

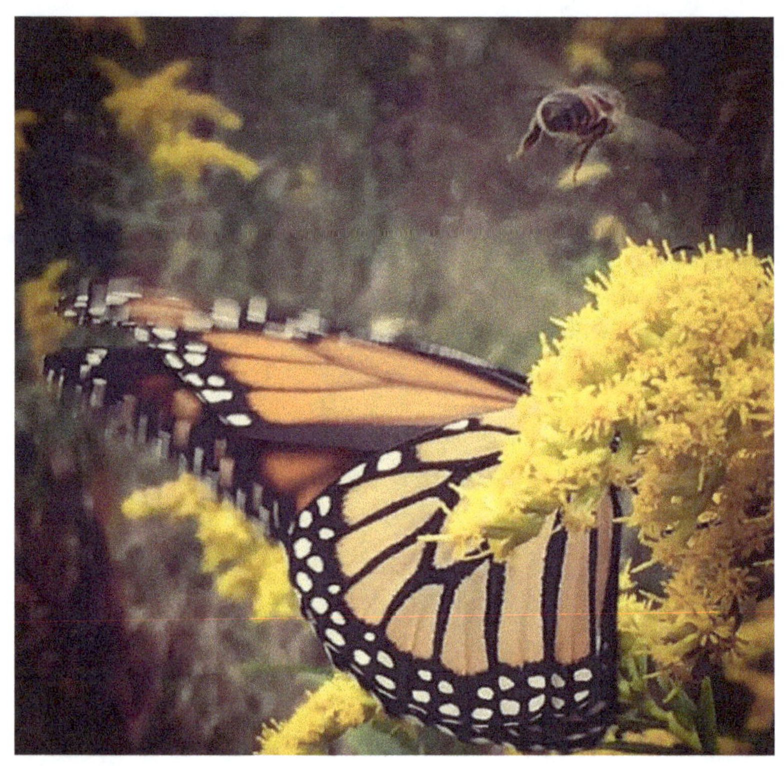

MARIA SURRICCHIO

Not What They See

21

Suited and pomaded, my parents shine
with fifties' glamor in the photo

where they lean through a window,
cheeks touching.

                   In that picture
my mother at sixty is not sealed

behind glass in a cancer unit
where she isolates for five days,

radium in her chest. The same
week, my father is not admitted

to the same unit, different floor.
Days later, he does not shuffle

to his greenhouse as if he's ninety,
not sixty-six. It is not the last time

he walks. He does not plant
cucumbers he will not see climb.

                   In that picture,
sun does not stream into the living

room where they lie, first one, then
the other. There is no hospital bed

by the window there.
In the yard, cucumbers do not press

against the glass for want of water.
They do not taste bitter.

MARYBETH RUA-LARSEN

Supermoon

Leaving the hospital
I come face to face
with fire and ice.
Only the moon
could manage it,
a canary singing
in this December snow,
setting the sky aflame
while my white breath
fogs the windshield.
And weren't we like this?
Opposites in everything –
you house proud, never
a sticky spot
on the kitchen floor,
and me with piles
everywhere
and cat-scratched
furniture.
I know
you weren't ready
to leave,
and this moon
you now inhabit –
burning, burning,
our house
on fire– is close enough
that I can almost
touch you.

CATHY MCARTHUR PALERMO

Mourning

Clouds lead me, faster than my elevated train.
I hold on, following the dead--

runaways in the last car—my brother
with our cousin tugging at his shirt,

we race through stations,
over rooftops, through crowded towns,

the sun to my right a drooping lily,
my brown hair lifted in air, as we plummet,

the train suddenly stopping,
emptying me on a platform in the middle

of Flushing. I've lost them
and don't know where I'm going.

The other night a tornado
spinning, removed what was familiar--

pin oak and red maple trees
split, stop signs uprooted.

A woman kneeling
in prayer in the street

who looked like my dead grandmother,
waved as I got on the last running bus.

Hours before, my father called
to say he drew our lineage tree.

When I arrive in his hospice room
on Birch Street, he is resting

in his bed, his newly shaved face staring up
to a gated window.

CATHY MCARTHUR PALERMO

Leaving

A girl on a cell phone claimed, *I have to go. I was supposed to be there this morning.*

I arrived by train to the city. Two policemen blocked the exit. I was thinking about my lost brown jacket that matched my jogging pants. Nothing usually matches.

Real horses...I could go anywhere, you bellowed and raced to the long line of riders on the hill. Someone tossed you a helmet. You had no breakfast. I waved; two hours later took your photo on a white horse named Troubles. After lunch you left, following the Intermediates.

My mother gave me boxes of photographs with no dates. She didn't know them, father's relatives: a man with a mustache in a suit and bow tie, a woman with a long, frilly dress, hair down to her knees. Negatives too, I held up to light. In a cemetery, I saw photos of people who wore water-colored shirts, jewelry.

In Cornell's print, a woman peers from a photo, a window. The ship is leaving the harbor. The city in weep holes, windows, like Hitch-cock's.

The week my brother died, I drifted in a rowboat. He said was going upstate, he didn't want my split pea soup.

We were all living in Queens, half lying; the bridge connecting us.

JENNIFER FRANKLIN

After the Funeral

Transparent in this black dress,
my breasts are disappearing,

becoming less minatory.
Unable to stand side-glancing,

you made it impossible to crack
autumn or walk this ice charade.

I am street lamps, iron rail planted
deep in cement. In your closet,

with your clothes and books piled
beside me-wrapped and labeled—

Mama with her face. I salvage
your locket and shut your photograph

between its little doors. It hides
under my dress, imprints

my blotched skin, small and precise—
marking me yours. My mouth

is starved of longing words. No one
speaks of you. At night, I covet

your morphine. To swallow the dull liquid
would satisfy. In darkness, I wait

to be laid out in the cold room
where it's not permitted to sing

or recline. I cannot undress.
Your smell hangs in the air

and cannot be banished by all
the open windows in the world.

ALEXIS DAVID

Block-Printed Apple Linen

Lindsey P. Butterfield block prints apples next to apples.

I am wearing a red cotton dress.

The milk in the fridge grows weary from the summer heat.

I bought a forest last month.

I dig deep into the soil and pull out metal mattress springs.

It is not that we die, because we don't.
We turn.

Apple into cotton into milk into dirt.

JENNIFER BARBER

Antiphon: Spring Leaves

You rustle like the pages
of a newspaper
but, not knowing how to read,
you have no idea
       that yesterday a star
swallowed a planet
          as big as Jupiter,
the whole thing recorded by a camera.

You don't know
that scientists predict
the sun will swallow Earth in four billion years
after drying up
         our rivers, lakes, and seas.

You don't know. I don't want you to.
Just keep doing
       what you've always done,
letting go in fall,
leafing out in spring,
       each of you emblazoned on the sky
like a sunlit psalm,
         a green belief.

JENNIFER BARBER

Antiphon: Wind

Today I unfasten you
from the clothesline where
some celestial being hung you to dry.
The grass sweetens. The clover blooms.
I fold you into smaller
and smaller squares.

**EVEN LEAVES HAVE
STORIES TO TELL**

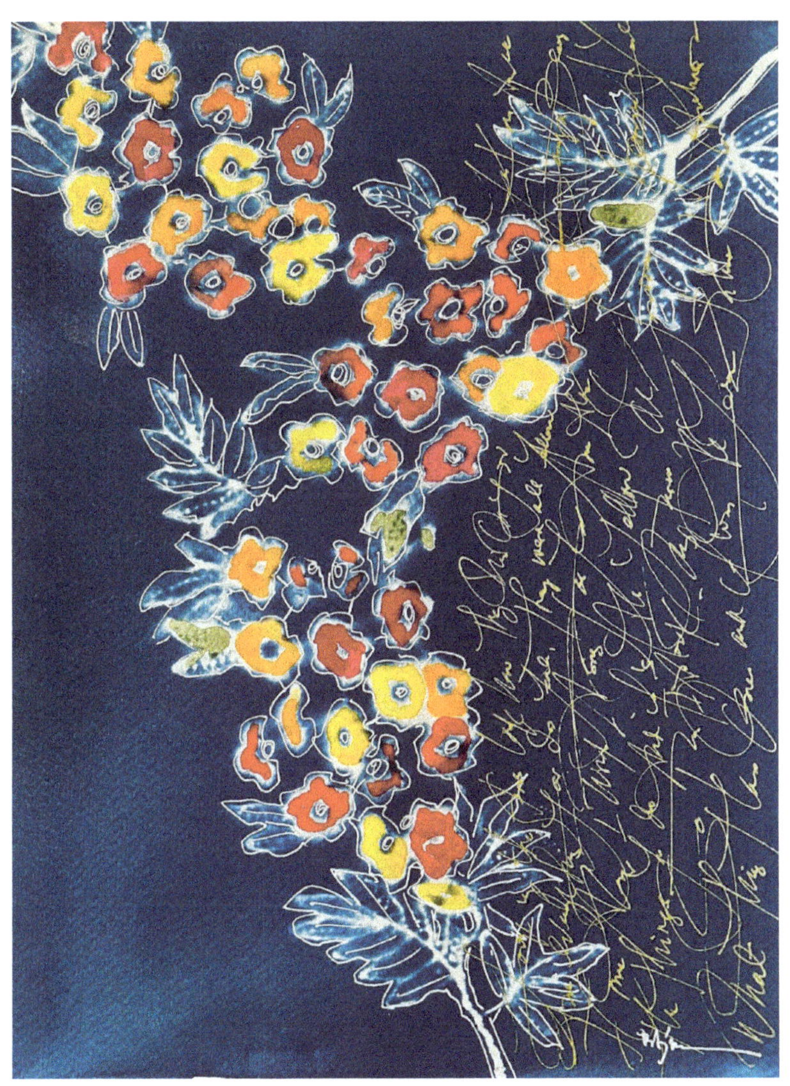

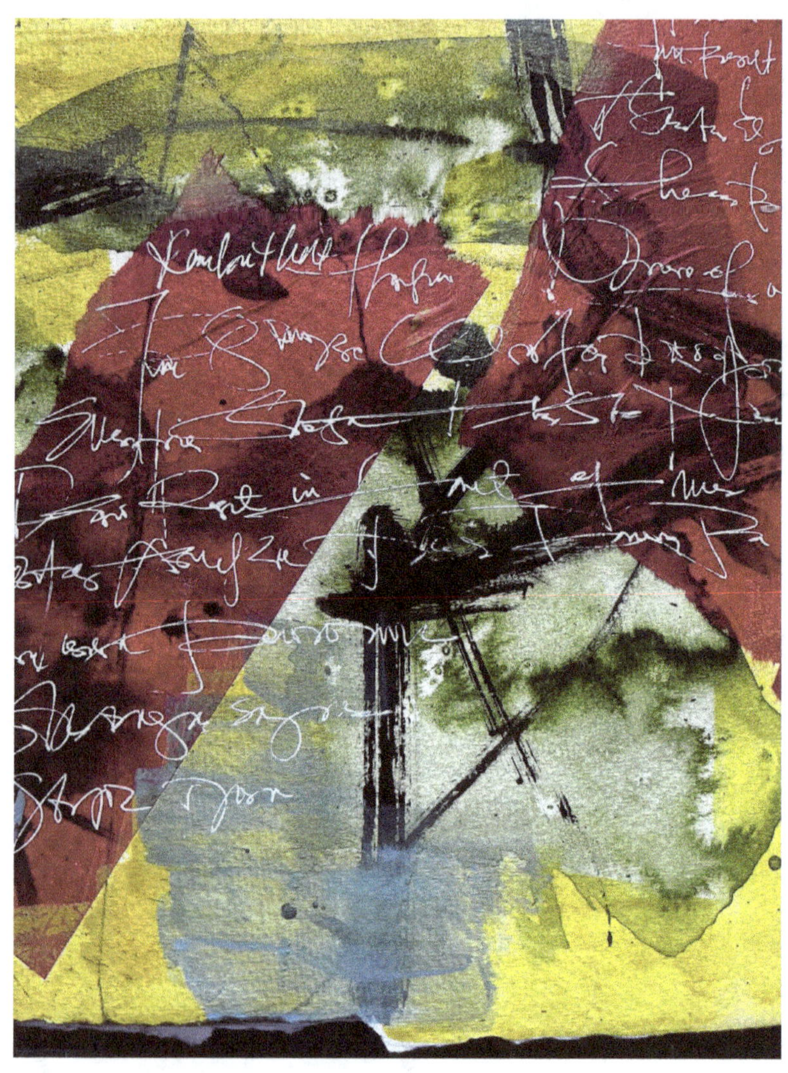

SRI SOEKARMOEN MCCARTHY   **UNTITLED ASEMIC WRITING**

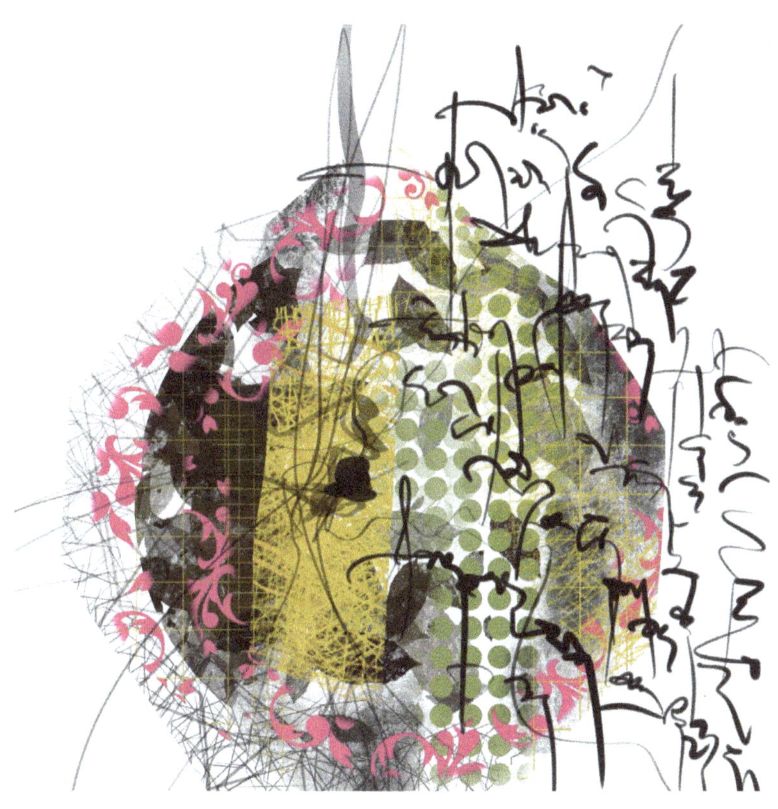

MOIRA MAGNESON

Foreclosure

A house full of flies this morning,
hundreds padding the windowpanes,
pacing the rim of shot glasses,
spelunking into trash. Masters
of the preliminary, they zip past
zithering the air in flashy black
suits, fast on the way to somewhere,
an appointment with somebody
always in their calendar. Watch them
circumnavigate the continuum
of town cars, trains, & taxis, humdrum
conversation circling the offal & bones
of the market news, multiocular eyes
on the prize—the rise & fall Dow
Jones of the body. See how they hurry
at this early hour, dazzled by biomass
stink, tumescent sweet & sour mash
of the house on the brink of collapse.
They'll drink to you, hedging the closing
deal, the final breath, loving you
best when you're at your death.

AMANDA SHAW

Past Perfect

An oleaginous rainbow
floats in the heat
on puddles in the Safeway lot.

Anchor no more, Don Lemon's
muddled his cocktail a bit too long.
If I'm honest, Don, implies you're not.

I've curated this body for mirrors.
My feet are hot, I want something sweet,
the flies are buzzing for rot.

RYAN HARPER

Waltz for Judy

If we do not seduce her, she will laugh at us.

Leading men tend to die
from the heat before the camp
turns cool. Hair piled high,
a sunburst cinch, and she is out
the gate—velvet gloves,
rougebloom, collar of lace,
bodice beads graggering—
fighting beauty, country real.

On her way, men with issues
jabber in cut time, hooters
and gawkers in seared fields,
crackling as the splintered wood
of carnivals in slow collapse,
decaying in the chase
of youth, straining against stayed light,
as if the sun forced accord
on the members—the parties,
the strides, the coordinated intimacies
of conflict, festooned.

At least today, she, together
with a mission, will pace them
to their carousing end.
A touch with the scepter top
obscured, feel for the deceit
of wine—clang goes the last dish,
lace, starch, and she is through
the last door, alone with the master
of ceremonies. Quick frisson,
but a tug of the sleeve and her blood
rewarms. The party has ended,
the camp has cooled;
time to turn another head.

RYAN HARPER

Waltz for Ruth

Whither thou goest I will go.

Two at work
atop the till

The reaper slopes dorsal
over the harrowed, pulse
of ocher in the bowing, arms
circle thick, windward
bout of spruce, impasto
shapes a harvest,
shapes to come.

The thresher lofts the given
flail to the grain, sweeps
across the gold body, glazing
glissando ribbons skyward
in dissolution, cereal
for the picking.

A drift, a plain
exchange of souls

RYAN HARPER

The Winding Tower

The old giant knows the dance:
standing braced and longing
for withdrawal the body
goes cabling, *tendu*

à la seconde, straightened
gearing mordant grinding
ankles, recruits the muscles
aligned over the core.

With closing labor the giant
holds, locked *allongé*,
until the green hills wrinkle
away the silent transformers

tipple corps to new devices:
freeze of poppet, stuck
the avatar, bolted but bending
before the next stiff wind.

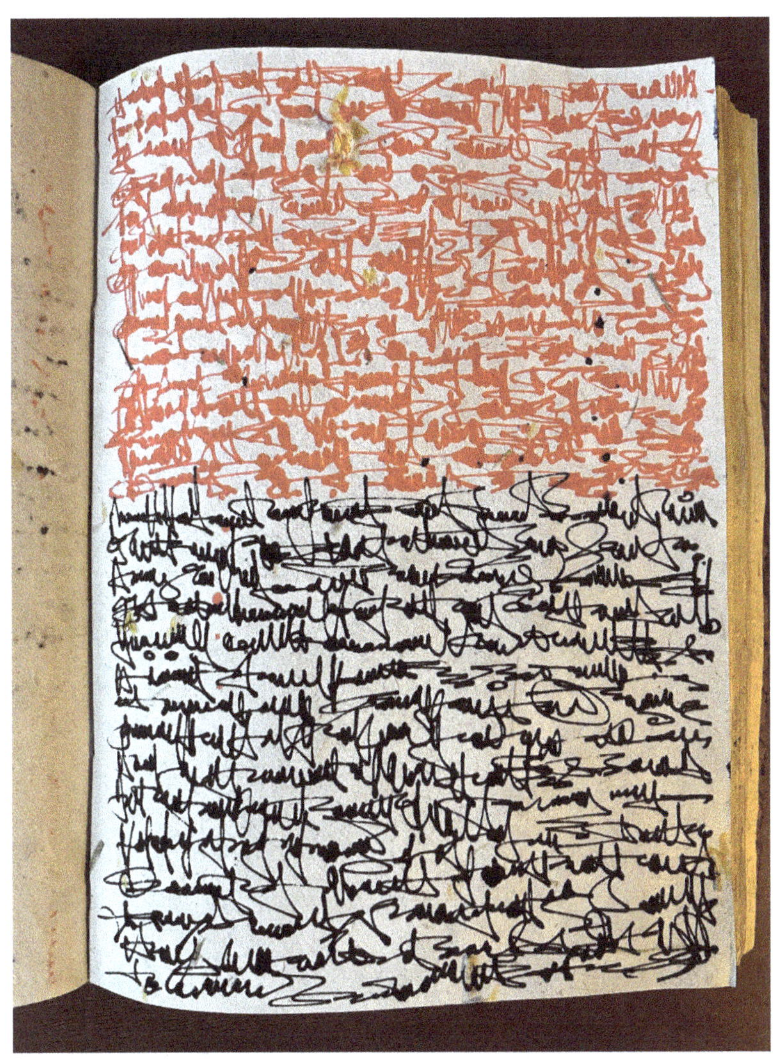

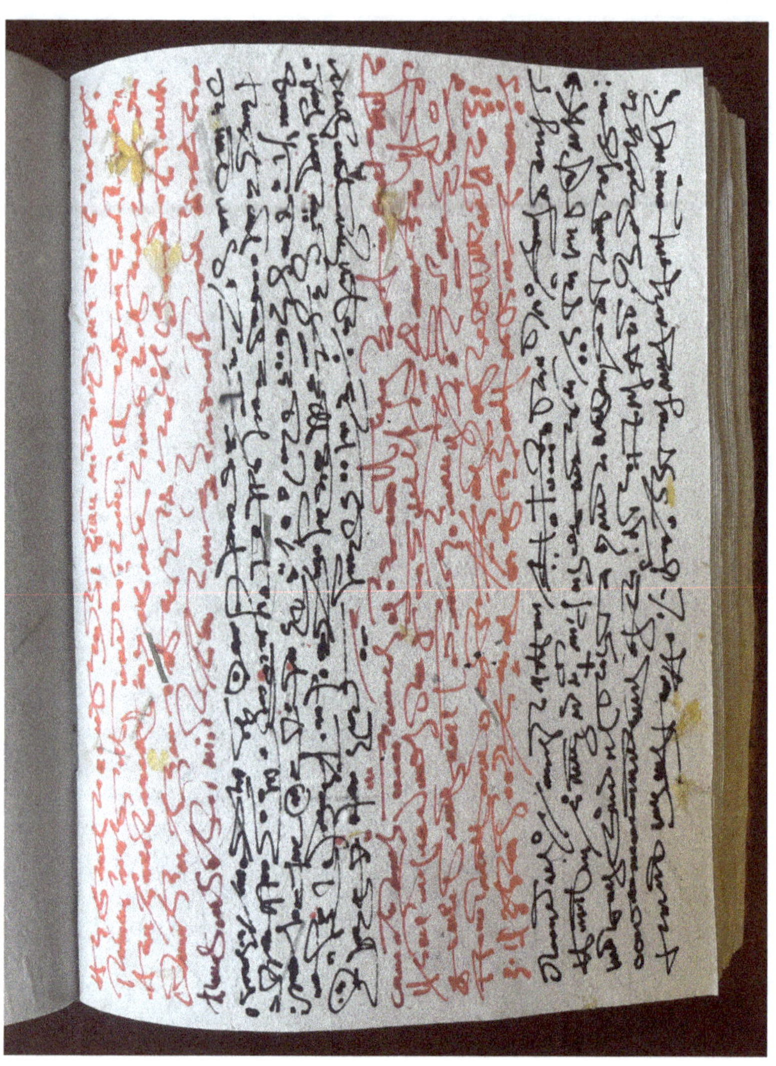

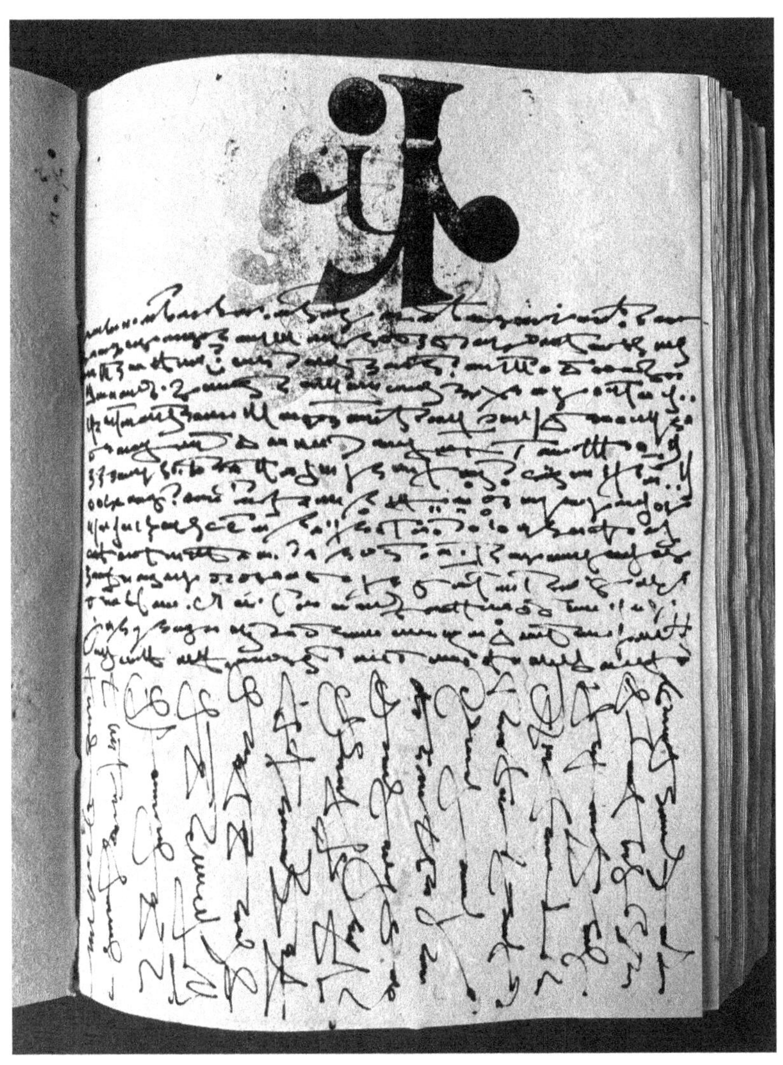

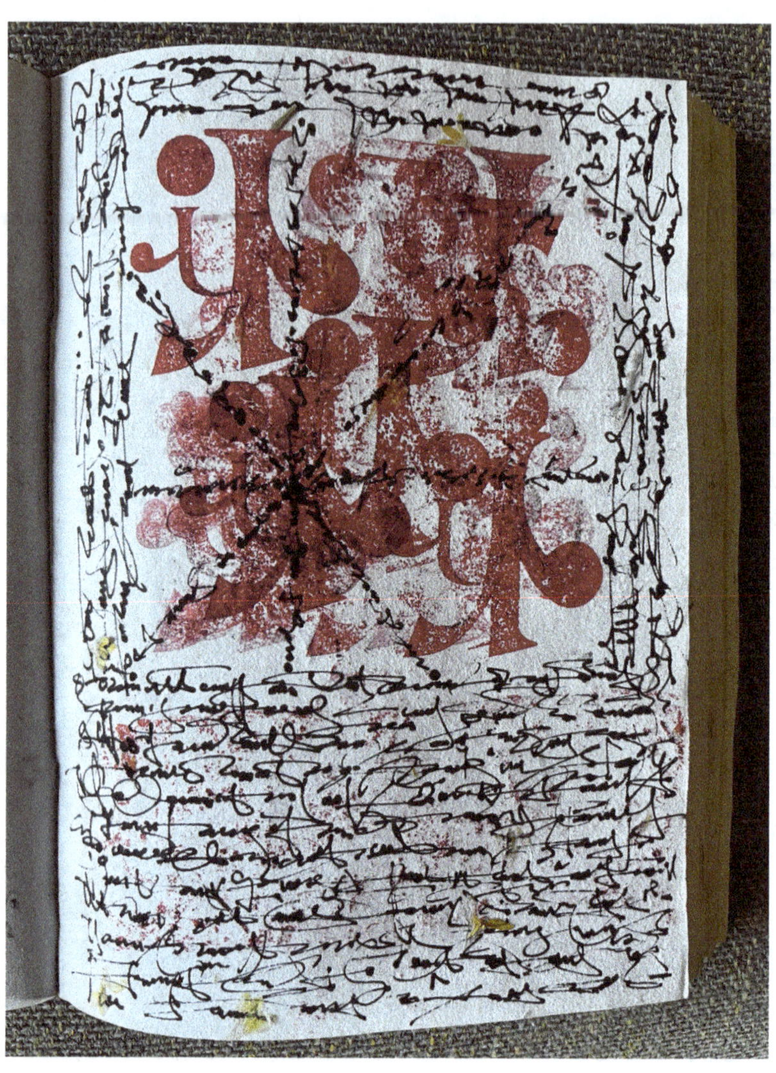

CHRISTINE JONES

Forgiveness

A windblown daffodil withholding its bloom, carries on
all season. I arrange my desires in a vase, each stem leans
into a distant view where they become dune grass. Spirit
means wind means air means breath means I'm learning
to imagine I exist as a gull skimming the ocean, see above
& below & love. Even when.

ELIZABETH MERCURIO

The Magdalen Girls

I was able to use my voice to make the devil fall asleep.
—Sinéad O'Connor

A sweet song in your Dublin garden.
no.
a scream.
a testament.

like Kahlo's wounded deer:
this is how you sing, ripped by grief.

you said the tears didn't stop
for twenty-five years—
& I am singing too.

this is why we speak to you, confide in you
we unrepentant Magdalens

the demons are asleep now.

rest well angel.

HEATHER TRESELER

'Everyone in me is a bird'

After Anne Sexton's "In Celebration of My Uterus"

In protest of the clinical vogue
that advised middle-aged women
still beset by blood but done with children
to retire sexual organs, Sexton wrote:
"There is enough here to please a nation."

The surgeon, in a blue skull-cap, stands
poised to fashion from the midlife
body something sleek and mid-century
modern: to tidy up the flood before
the pause, to cage the ache in the fabled

monstrous matron. But why silence
what hums in self-contenting song?
This organ, we are told, is the size
of a fist. In half the nation, a muscle
thought capable, culpable of crime.

Sexton found no felon in her womb,
its drum set, its estrogen rock band,
resisting mustachioed Prosperos
who sought to curb *dowagers' lust*—
lest there be unseemly scenes,

trouble in the marriage bed, a florid
affair, a *late child mistake*. Let women
remain lawns, men the roving rakes?
We still have need of a new
philosophy. To claim, as inalienable,

the property of the body. If pleasure
is a barter, let its horizon be
one's own. Consider Brueghel's
"Winter Landscape with Skaters
and a Bird Trap," where the starlings

are not ornaments but gravities—
as live as Sexton was once, as free,
as fated as the skaters skirting death
above frozen water: what craves flight,
crowning sky. Declaring itself, I.

EILEEN CLEARY

Beginning with a Quote by Anne Bradtreet or Lines Immortalized in the Mirror

I am obnoxious to each carping tongue
Who says my hand a needle better fits.

Page and pen long favor men, let's admit,
over women of equal ink. These same women

tote prattling toddlers to minivans, scan for wolves
after stringing shifts as second fiddles.

Must they wonder how they'll be savaged,
plump their exquisite bodies lest they attract?

One summer, in Holbrook, a man closed in on me,
pushed me into a roadside ditch. Quarter

mile from my home; it could have been any distance.
And he might have tracked any to attack.

Same man on the news next week after
pommeling someone else. Baton passed in night

zones *mano a mano.* And wasn't this poem
about women's words, sans hand over mouth,

past the binary 1600's, men vs. women, men
vs. Eve's sin, men vs. life-size dummies, vs. unschooled manikins.

Anne, did you refer to a better fit?

Oh my! Women's words bog the gut and glut the mind.
She needs a list of reputable topics: man, god, child.

Nothing too wild. Nothing too gentle. For all that's holy,
nothing sentimental. If in a poem, a man finds

a naked starling, its gaping orange hunger,
he's free to fashion feeding sticks from coffee straws,

but a woman must bury that darling. She must
not coddle the offspring of her feeble brain,

her thoughts tripped before the front door's frame.
Must men be men, and women have no claim?

A man writes of love in ruins, crumbling
architecture in his chest. Such fidelity.

For this to be self-pity, he would be she.
If she'd only obey, she'd be given more say.

Today, another poet vanished, her voice
vanquished in plain sight. Honor

the godly hunter who mounted her
on the wall with a pushpin through her throat.

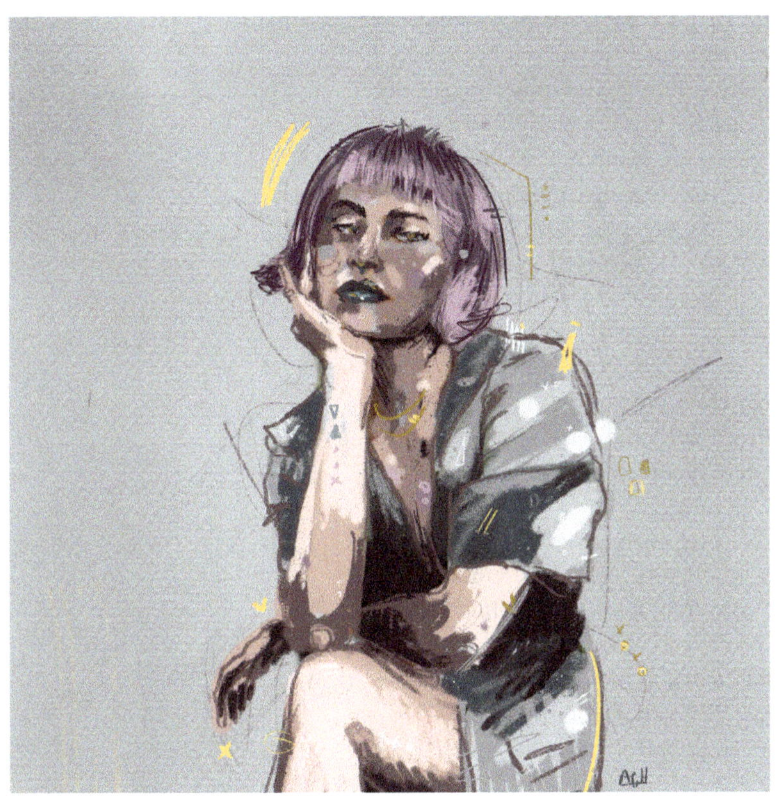

JEANNE MARIE BEAUMONT

Nursing

At their end, the women had come
back around to doll-play. Some were
hoarders; it was known if no babies
were to be found in the common room
to search their beds and drawers. Tiny ones
and life-size, ones with soft bodies
and hard heads, with malleable bodies
and sleep-eyes, with bottles and booties,
bibs and onesies. Clothes would be lost
then reappear, swapped about, mis-
matched. Regularly they were sanitized
by the staff and set aright before passing
again from lap to cradling arm.
                              So it was
that I delivered from my closet's far top
a small half-cloth-bodied infant named
Penny, doubtless for her thatch of copper-
blond synthetic hair, that my mother
had given to me claiming she looked
just like baby-me. After I'd kept her
for near half a century, I brought back
to my mother, and the others too, this
refound Penny, where she joined the nursery
of the nameless, unrecognized now by her,
as was I, as was any.

ASHLEY KUNSA

Offline

Somewhere, I am still fifteen. My wrist still woven in friendship, baby
fat unthieved from my cheeks. Nothing has been

broken yet, or can be. The path to the forgotten
farmhouse in the woods becomes a path only because we make it so,

our Reeboks careless on the crisp grass, our laughter announcing us
to man and beast alike. T and C, up ahead, their hair blonde and long

down backs not yet marked by summer; distracted, I lag,
the strap of my mother's 35mm carving a ravine into tender shoulderflesh.

Just over the sunken threshold, waterchoked mattresses, dishes clotted with some
not-so-distant dinner's remains, six matching Yellow Pages, vintage 1969.

Those were the best days of our lives.
When sound spills out from somewhere beyond the scene, only

C lifts her head in the direction of the shot, and only for an instant.
This is not the story where we are eaten. We do not barely escape

with our lives. Nothing is lost but hours under the trees' ignorant canopy, nothing taken
but the late afternoon light unspooled across floorboards,

a photo for a school assignment. We understand threat but not enough
to feel threatened. These are the Pennsylvania suburbs,

and the year is 1997. America is only just coming online.

PAMELA WAX

This Small, Wide World

I hear the side door of her truck slide open across the street & think *mail.* I flash on Meg
Ryan & that restaurant scene, & my own last climactic delivery. Wrong film, I know, but

with the click of our mailbox lid, I think of hand-written notes & holiday missives no one
writes anymore, the sympathy cards Hallmark doesn't make for job loss or climate grief,

those thin blue envelopes from pen pals in Kenya & Israel I lost touch with & can't find
on Facebook, but whose stamps I steamed off & saved. Through the window I watch Bertie

head up the hill, lean & tan, her telltale button-up the same blue as those bygone
aerogrammes—& unwrinkled—a bundle of mail in her arms. I imagine hail & sleet,

global warming, the pandemic, how she shows up though it was never the USPS motto, how
Herodotus wrote that about the Persians in 500 BCE, including the word *gloom* on his list

of what could never deter such speedy couriers. When she's out of sight, I open the front
door, reach into the mailbox adorned with a #SaveThePostOffice sticker I got from MoveOn

to show her love thirty-three American crises ago. Among the junk, a glossy 6x9.
I've just retired, but for a blink of my eye, I consider applying, usps.com/careers. *Sense*

of service to the community. Diverse workplace. When I was twelve, I asked about a summer
job at the local post office. The clerk said I was too young for civil service, & besides,

I should set my sights higher. Higher? I thought. I show my husband the ad, tell him how I
need to be of service. Oh, yeah? he says, leading me upstairs. I hear Bertie start her truck

to drive away. Someone down the block may receive a colorful stamp from a faraway land.
I conjure the ride-through at the World's Fair when I was four. *It's a small world* is wide

and glorious and I want it—a safari in Kenya, a close-up of a blue-footed boobie
in the Galápagos, a pilgrimage on the El Camino, a tête-à-tête with the Dalai Lama

in Dharamshala. But my husband wants to keep it local, like our vegetables, wishes
for a world so small & intimate, that all I'd want to do is deliver his mail.

MICHAEL J. CARTER

Morticia Adams Pens a Letter

It is not surprising to Gomez and me
that you can see the radiation
pulsing blue waves into your brain.
It is also no surprise that you
can now smell the radiation though you believe
that the scent of BBQ and burning leaves
emit from your overactive imagination.
I'm not so sure. Your ability to perceive
what others cannot is surely inherited from Uncle Fester
with his 1000-watt smile, an open current
lodging deep into your DNA. You are as rare
as the bull sharks pulled from the Mississippi
in your native Iowa and just as far from your natural habitat.
We have missed you so. As discerning people
we both understand what radiation exposure will do
to a person: Gozilla and Mothra, Peter Parker's
transformative spider, the 50 Foot Woman,
the Teenaged Werewolf. I can't wait to see
what's next for you, a mild-mannered librarian
becomes, what? The Atomic Archivist? Dewey Decimal?
Circadia the Wild Cataloger? A world of possibilities.
No matter what happens you'll always have a home
with us. What's your pleasure? A night of cards with Thing,
the bed of nails in the dungeon, visiting up the chimney
with Cousin It, the cave and swamp with Wednesday
and Pugsley, cooking up potions with Grandmama?
Or maybe you'll just cuddle up in the window seat
with a book, nestled in Kitty's mane. All you need to do
is show up and ring the bell. Lurch will show you in,
take your hat and carry in your luggage. I'll be arranging roses
to welcome you back. I'm beheading them as we speak,
the stems and thorns revealed, so beautiful this time of year.

KYLE POTVIN

This is Serious

Dan McGinn: Can you teach somebody to be funny?
Jerry Seinfeld: Nope.
> —Harvard Business Review

why are you laughing
a bumble bee is giving birth
      to the last of the species

sumac is raging
against the aging oaks
      or are they maples

the world is limping by
river tide in out
      when I least expect it

I consume use   eat
burrata ripe tomatoes salt
      a swirl of fruity olive oil

why does *fruity*
autocorrect
      to *guilty*?

human   I laugh
too easily
      am I funny

the nuns from my childhood
would say no
      that girl never smiled

DEVON BALWIT

This Trend Must Be Stopped

Gussied up, the maple looks goofy. Googly eyes,
please, as if fall's flush, death's fire in the blood,
were insufficient adornment. Should anyone try that
with me, Elmo slippers or Teletubby jammies,
consider this poem power of attorney and restore me
my threadbare dignity. Better the rain hammer
every last leaf to the ground with the iciness
of a mercenary guarding the sole working runway—
You, you, and you will not rise to tomorrow's sky.
I tread apologetically over the fallen as I recognize
kin. Crows gust left to right in ragged companies.
True is the ugly bolus on the naked trunk, the puffed
scar of the missing limb. True the sodden
shoe and the clogged gutter. If I want solace,
I'll have to claw it from the season with a rake.

GEORGE YATCHISIN

First Principles

Why learn to write when you can take

a papermaking class,

                why muck about

with pulp when it's simpler it seems

to plant a tree.

             Everyone who has had

a photo taken at the Grand Canyon's rim

has jokily acted as if

                they backed up too far

and then dropped into the depths, a scene-

stealer for sure.

             Like everyone you will forget

the Colorado River has been busy

six million years

             carving, a word too

hard for something closer to lovers' hands

gently letting each other go,

                  but not too far.

ROBERT WITMER

The Siren

A little girl calls to a cat
On the opposite bank
Of a canal, a river really, running
Through the city's concrete straitjacket,
Not wide, but wide enough.
Sweetly, so sweetly, she calls,
Her eyes serene. Come,
Come kitty, come here, come to me,
Come to me here.
So sweet is her voice.
The deaf water running fast.

BARBARA SIEGEL CARLSON

Marking the Place

You come with a notebook and pen to sit on a bench on a hill. It's
November, midday and you are alone in a foreign country. But not
really alone. People live down in the valley, only you can't see them.
You write something in your notebook. A breeze sends a shiver
through the reddish weeds. You hear the tower bell gong twelve times.
Then take a black napkin out of your pocket. There's a stain in the
corner. You're not sure where the napkin came from or who you were
with, or if you will ever come here again. You put it on a blank page
in your notebook like the wind you have no words for.

COLE SWENSEN

Twilight

We're on a terrace looking out over a river, though a terrace is always more its view than itself. And a view expands whatever sees it, and whatever sees it grows to be it. We stayed out on the terrace until late in the evening, or at least we seemed to, leaving, as we did, bodies behind that went on talking lightly and warmly and admiring the view.

COLE SWENSEN

Owls and Edges

An owl cares only about edges—you can see it any evening—all di-shevelling—grading by degrees, and as the darkness progresses, so do the edges. And each one is a wing. It may not belong to any given thing, but the owl tends to gather them, being the night-gleaner, the gatekeep-er, and therefore responsible for strays.

Stray wings are a problem all over the world, and a danger because if they all get together, which they seem likely to do, and soon, they'll cover the sky enough to block out the sun, and just imagine the harm that that will do—though that is not their goal—that's not what they want at all—they just want to talk—to know how you are, to ask about your life, how it's going, and to exchange a few pleasantries, about the weather, for instance, and then they'll sigh and agree that it's been pretty gloomy lately.

COLE SWENSEN

The Man Who Cried

It was at a sad movie—more moving than sad, really—that a young man, 23 years old, began crying, and it wasn't that he couldn't stop; he just didn't. And though when they first met him, people often asked him why he was crying, he never had much of an answer, so they just moved on to other things. Early on, he proved to be an extremely gifted scientist and, crying, made important discoveries in particle physics, married a prominent psychoanalytic theorist, had three children and several grandchildren, and, still crying, became an accomplished pianist in his later years, playing late into the night before crying himself to sleep.

Advent in Time of War

Behold the bespoke billboard attorney
oozing glib competence over folded arms
onto a weedy urban lot.

What is left to litigate?

I have learned of a dearth of Mall Santas
this season—makes sense—
at sixty-plus and overweight
they were such a high-risk cohort
in those first pandemic waves.

Veni, Emmanuel, veni.

O come, flitter down, you butterfly Monarch,
for some of us still strew milkweed seeds
across this butchered planet.

LISA J. SULLIVAN, ART EDITOR

INTERVIEW WITH VISUAL ARTIST, BETTE RIDGEWAY

It is my pleasure to introduce to our readers the celebrated visual artist Bette Ridgeway, who currently creates in Santa Fe, New Mexico. For nearly 50 years, her art has been exhibited globally in over 80 prestigious venues, including Palais Royale in Paris, Kobayashi Gallery in Tokyo, and at the Embassy of Madagascar. Ms. Ridgeway is the recipient of many awards, most recently the 2023 Leonardo DaVinci International Prize, 2022 Paris International Prize, and the 2022 Michelangelo International Prize. She was also named a Top 60 Contemporary Master and has permanent collections housed in the Mayo Clinic and Federal Reserve Bank. Ms. Ridgeway has written extensively about art in publications such as *Monk Magazine*, *LandEscape Art Review* (Special Edition), and the *London Art Biennale*. We are delighted to publish six of her stunning works in this issue of *Lily Poetry Review* and thankful for the time she spent completing this interview.

Q: Bette, you are best known for large-scale, poured canvases using acrylic paints and describe your technique as "controlled improvisation" and "layering light." Without giving away any trade secrets, can you give us some insight into your process?

A: First, I want to thank you, Lisa, for the privilege of this interview for your outstanding journal. I'm impressed not only with its content, but with the superb graphic design.

About my process: it is very simple. No secrets. I pour the paint on the canvas, instead of using a brush. The tricky part is how I control each pour using various supports to shape the canvas. Over these five decades I have refined the technique and it continues to grow and change.

Q: You had the honor of being mentored by the acclaimed Abstract Expressionist Paul Jenkins for three decades. Can you tell our readers how that mentorship began and the most important things you learned from him?

A: I was introduced to Jenkins in 1978 by Jean Kennedy Smith who was the founder and chairperson of the National Committee Arts for the Handicapped. I was serving as its Executive Director and CEO. Jenkins had donated a beautiful poster as a fundraising tool for the organization. Mrs. Smith told him I was an artist and he responded by asking to see my work.

He kindly looked at my watercolors in 1979 and forcefully suggested that I was a colorist. He implored me to remove the subject matter and focus on color, time, and space. It took me nine years to figure out HOW to do that. He never taught me or showed me how to accomplish this; however, he was kind enough to review my slides. Remember the Kodak Carousel? I went through hundreds of miles of canvas and gallons of paint during those years. I told myself that my studio was a laboratory – a laboratory in which to try everything without judgment. People thought I was behaving like a mad scientist, as I was so driven. I still have dozens of journals from those days. I wrote as I worked… critiqued every painting with a stern eye.

My local library in Arlington, Virginia, had an extensive library of art books – art history, art technique. I took five books home every week and read them all, making notes in my journals. That was a very intense period. Painting, studying, writing, and analyzing other artists' work.

In 1988, I sent a series of slides of my new work to Jenkins. He said, "You are ready for a show." I nearly passed out. I guess I was doing something right! Ha.

His encouragement gave me the impetus to take my portfolio around to galleries. One beautiful contemporary gallery in Alexandria, Virginia, asked to keep my portfolio for a few days. Remember in those days, portfolios were photographs. We had to shoot the painting, have the film developed, and pray that the colors would come out perfectly.

After a few days, that Alexandria gallery, FOTA, called and asked if I could be ready for a show in one month. One of their artists had backed out and they needed to fill a prime time slot. Of course I said yes. Then I worked around the clock and prepared 22 large paintings for the show.

At the opening, people were lined up around the block. A gorgeous invitation had been sent to the gallery's collectors. Paul sent an enormous floral arrangement – in all white – with a note that read, "Break a leg." I still have that note tucked away.

Unbelievably, the show sold out…and that was the beginning. I learned that perseverance is almost more important than talent. Drive. Sweat. Tears. That's pretty normal. That solo show set me up for a long and rewarding career.

Q: Your work is categorized as the "second generation of Abstract Expressionism." What, in your mind, differentiates the work of the first generation (Paul Jenkins, Joan Mitchell, Franz Kline, Jackson Pollock, and others) from the second?

A: I have been described by gallerists and curators as a second-generation Abstract Expressionist. I will let others explain how my work fits into that category.

Q: Do you need to be in a certain mood or state of mind to paint? If so, what steps do you take to get there (i.e., to find your muse)?

A: I do a short meditation before the beginning of each day in the studio. The goal is to create an opening, a space, so that the image can come in. After setting up the canvas, I mix the colors in 9 oz. plastic cups. I put my entire focus on the colors and the density of the pigments. The density and the velocity of the pours are important to the success of the work. I allow myself to become one with the tools, the paint, and the canvas. My south-facing studio has magnificent clerestory windows and the light is spectacular. Often, I see that I am a channel. The work just comes through me.

Q: Have you ever collaborated with others? If so, can you describe a couple of those projects?

A: No, I have always worked alone except for one occasion. When I created a large public commission for the Boro Building lobby in Tysons, Virginia, in 2018, I did employ four individuals to work with me. The painting, a triptych, was 15 feet high by 21 feet wide. This was the biggest challenge of my life, and I consider it a miracle that it came out as planned. Details on this are found on my website.

Q: For me, your pieces exhibit hypnotic, rhythmic movement – terms one might also use to describe music. This prompts me to ask, do you ever listen to music while you paint, and does it influence your work? What genres/artists do you most often paint to?

A: Yes, I often listen to music. I actually create playlists that create certain moods.

Recently, however, I am preferring to work quietly to keep the silent dialog with the pigments. There is great beauty in the quiet. Especially in this "noisy" time in our history. I do strive for movement and ethereal feeling in the work. This is accomplished with very subtle layering and clean, clear transparent colors. It is astute of you to recognize this.

Q: Your bio indicates your mentor, Paul Jenkins, advised you to "eliminate subject matter" and also mentions your "lifetime journey of non-objective painting." These phrases bring to mind John Keats' theory of "negative capability" in writing, which he described as the capability of "being in uncertainties, mysteries, doubts, without any irritable reaching after facts and reason." Does Keats' theory resonate with you? If so, how do you dampen the mind's instinct to (1) analyze as you work; and (2) create with an end result in mind? Do you have any tips to share for managing/negating this type of anxiety and "trusting the process"?

A: I absolutely subscribe to Keats' theory. Since my work is highly intuitive, I suspend any notion of what the outcome will be. This keeps me open to every possibility. I stay with the unknown. The paint takes me where it wants to go. Take a look at the films that show my technique. You will see the "dance" that takes place. I think it takes "action painting" to the next level.

I say to art students, "Fire that committee in your head." Seriously, as artists work, we often think – who will like this, who will buy this, maybe I need to change my style…blah blah blah. Turn off that self-talk. If you are feeling anxiety, do something else. Go back to painting in a calm frame of mind. Trust in the process. Trust in your ability to pull it off.

Q: Approximately how long does it take for you to complete a painting?

A: Sometimes just a few days. Sometimes I roll up the canvas and go back in months later. It's amazing how different things look after they have been marinating for a while.

Q: As a follow-up, how do you know when a painting is complete?

A: It tells me. It also tells me its name.

Q: Do you ever work on more than one painting at a time?

A: Oh yes, all the time. I love working in a series, especially if there is a similar palette.

Q: You've traveled extensively throughout your career to study and teach. What places and/or cultures did you find most fascinating as relates to art? Did any particularly inspire your own craft?

A: I'd say that living in Tananarive, Madagascar, in the late '60s really opened my eyes to the color and culture of these lovely people. There is a reverence for life and for the land. The landscapes are stunning and the skies are pure magic. Almost as magical as the landscape and skies in New Mexico!

Q: Lastly, what message do you hope your amazing art brings to the world?

A: This too is very simple. I want my work to lift the spirit. If I'm lucky enough, the viewer will connect with a memory, a thought, or an emotion. They will see beyond the obvious and take a moment to reflect. Perhaps they will even be moved.

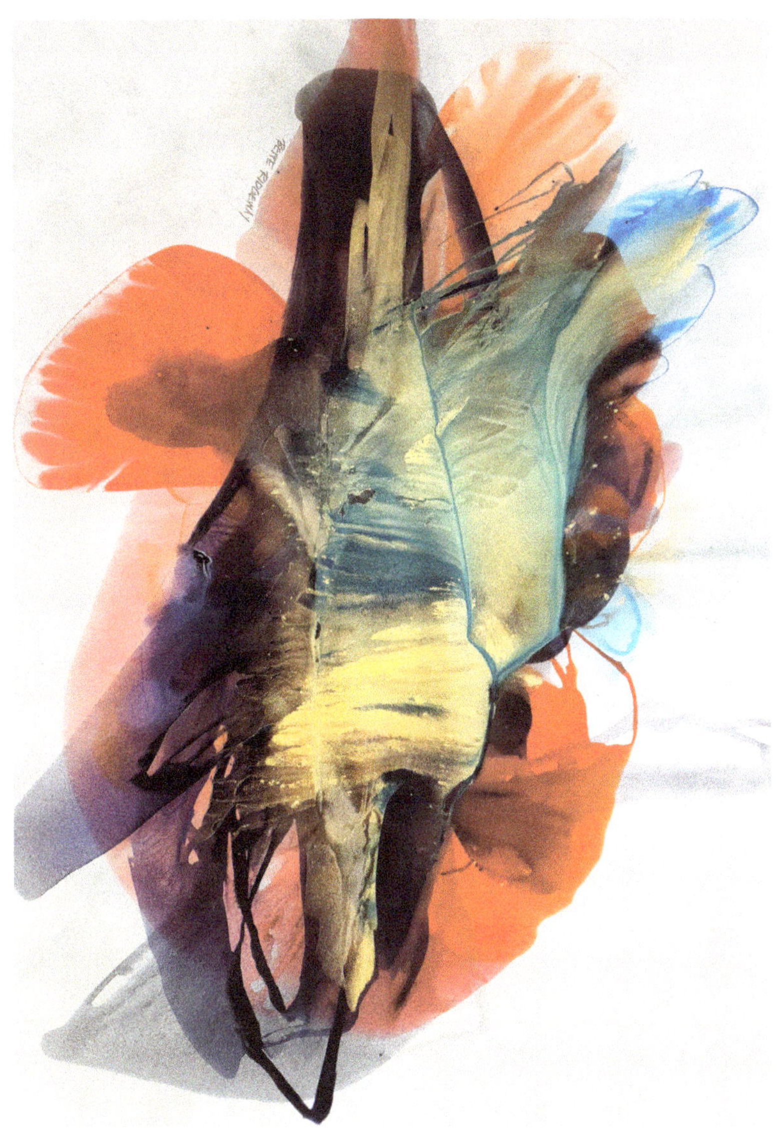

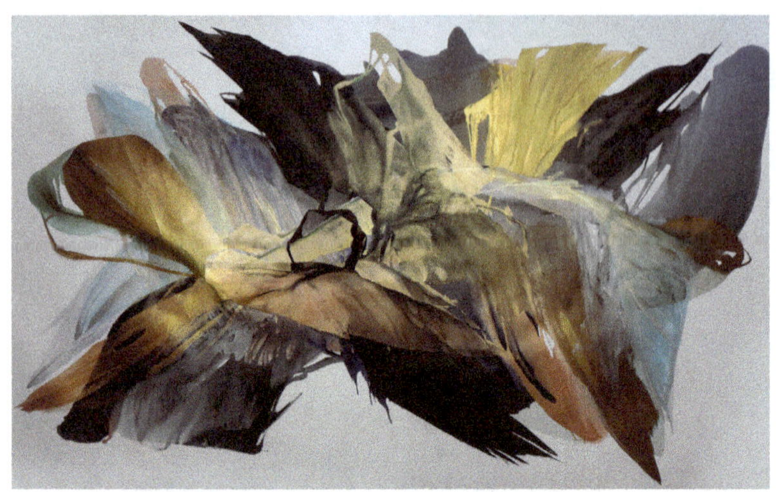

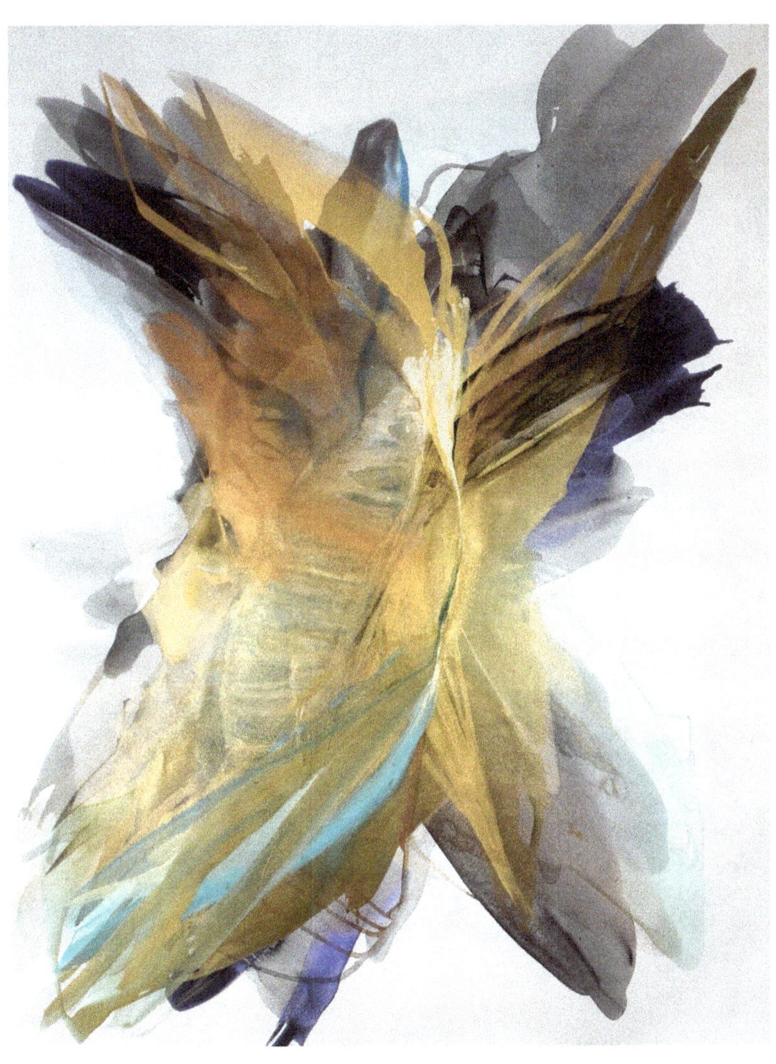

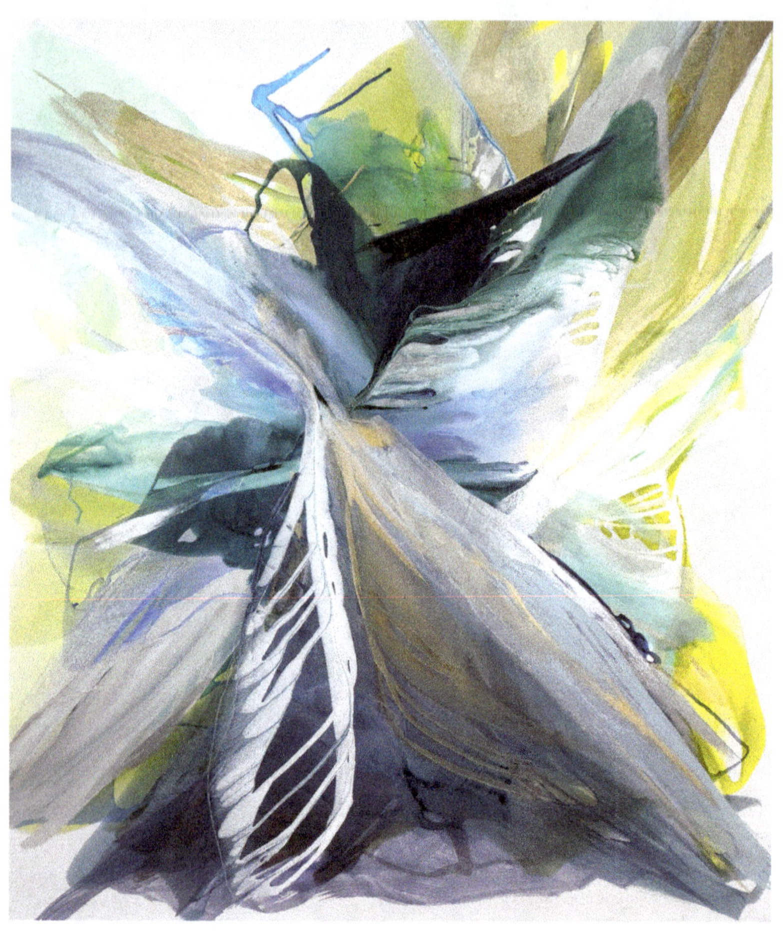

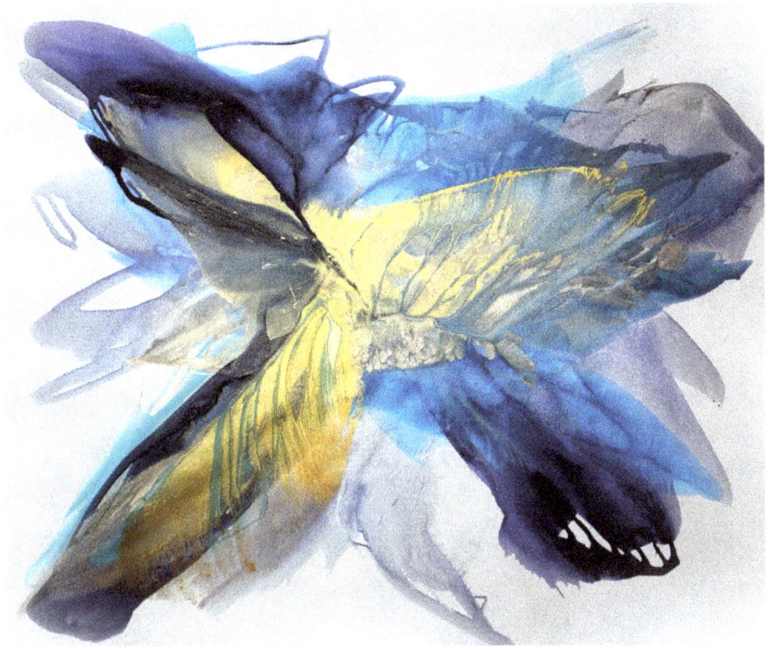

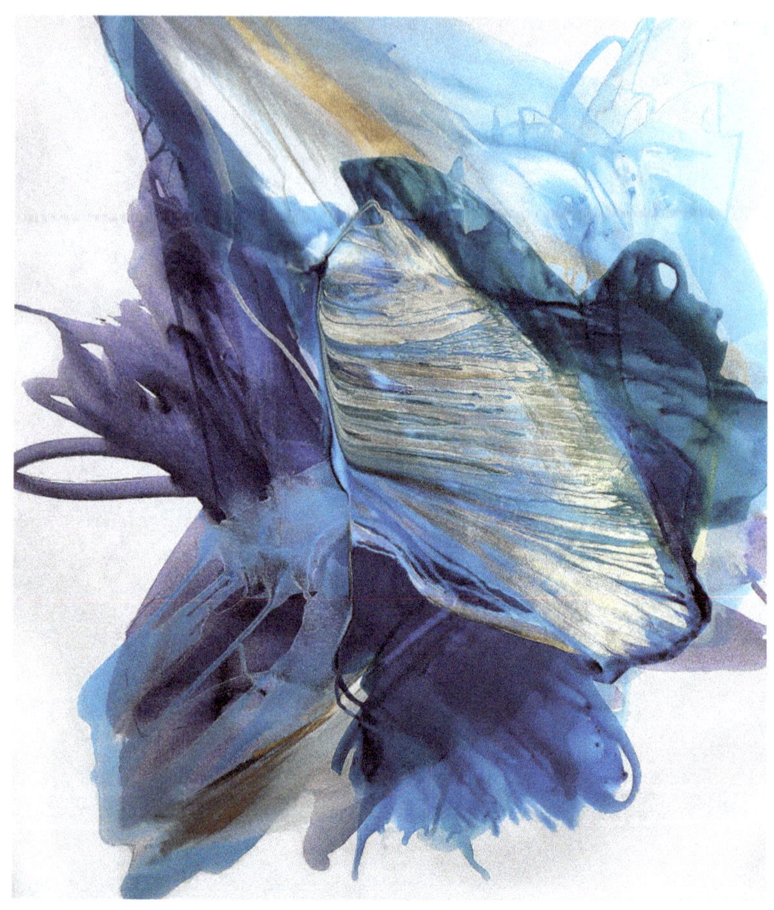

WENDY DREXLER

Field of Rocking Horses

—Ponyhenge, Lincoln, Massachusetts

They are never weary, the ponies, prancing their frozen spiral
        in a field of grass—forelegs tucked beneath them, hooves
                and heads held high, their molded plastic manes

                never stained by rain, their nostrils flaring. No one knows
        who brought them here: the sawhorse, boxy body painted
with blue stars; the black stallion, rearing on hind legs;

the pink, plush-tailed filly. Riderless, bridled and brindled, tooled,
        plastic saddles rest on sturdy metal stands or wooden rockers.
                Their children who loved them, loosened from their withers.

                This is not their story. I'm not sad today, it's October, crisp,
        clear, the maples still splendid, saturated in yellow coloratura.
And because the horses circle in place, none will tire. Because

this meadow has claimed them. Because sunlight dapples their shoulders.
        Because wind and rain have come and gone and will
                come again. Because they have known the press

                of thighs and have been loved, as I have been loved.
        Because they are fresh for the morning and for all after-
noon among the bobolinks that call out to each other and the tree

swallows swooping in and out of their nest boxes and the burst cattails
        that curry the sway of their backs. Because their work is no longer
                bearing and carrying. They have been let out of the mouth

                of years—the bay, the corduroy palomino, the sorrel, the dappled,
        the dun. And because they have weathered, they are of the house
of weather and of all the homes that I have weathered. And we are not yet rust.

CYNTHIA BARGAR

Atonement After Sunset at Ponyhenge

There is no thou to speak of.
—Lucie Brock-Broido

No burial for these beloved remains. No breath, no whinny,

No neigh. No dusty attic. No cellar, damp. No landfill.

No capture. No pasture grasses bolster molded stallions.

No saddle soap, no stable roses. No frills festoon the wooden

Ones on rocker rails, with tufts of straw for tails. No midway,

No corral, no pony pokey. No rough beasts slouching

Save for hobby horses & rocking ponies. No

Theologies but their rounding-the-bend mythologies.

        In their heyday I was young

& they were all the rage, yet I never wanted one.   Today, I

Pilgrim to the field where they circle. Praise their saviors,

Seek to redeem myself.   The sun sets.

It's the eve of tomorrow   sacred day.

        Are there not at least 100 ways to pray.

SANDY WEISMAN

Birds of Prey

I've given the falcon Botticelli eyes.

Clipped them from my book of Mary's,

pasted them on the bird's face, now rapturous.

From da Vinci I've lifted kind eyes

for the hawk, the eagle,

and stolen Mary's misgivings from Raphael,

glued them onto the barn owl

so she can listen to her heart:

> *Too hard, too hard,* she prays.

> *Give the job to the buzzard*

> *and let me sleep.*

LIBBY MAXEY

Turtle Sonnet

We surprise each other in the bluets; you
draw in, neglecting one rear leg—long-clawed,
pebbled black, dissuasion at your body's door.
I defer the field, resume my passing through,
a fearsome thing although unarmored, awed:
this hard-whorled quilt of shells from a fossil shore
crawled into modern June on living limbs
and met me. All praise, unfashionable God,
for this gray beauty, neither tuneful nor
rejoicing, shy Triassic antonym
            for more.

MAC STERN

the orange county three headed boy

He Speaks in Soliloquies [...eight, nine, ten]
His heartbeat Stings his Throat
He Peels his own Mouth like a rotting Persimmon
       sweet.

Every Night, his words glue themselves to the Floor Of My Mouth,
and Every Dawn, i scrub Them off when he isn't looking.
i leave him early, as if to say
      You have no power over me.

But his accents and inflections infect my day job,
      he can never know this, i think.
I count lists on a blue screen until my sight begins to wane
His voice is a softbox and it filters Certain Moments.
i shake him off,
It's a numbers game, and my eyes are grey.
I complete Actions in his Absence,
      banging drumsticks on subordinate's heads and calling it purposeful.

he lays In Bed and looks for Imprints of teeth and nails and Hard cheekbones
in the Crook Of His Neck,
Trying to calculate how long the empty space beside him felt wrong,
      trying to remember what
           monstrous form he
               conjured from his eyes.

I have have planned my own loving poorly,
now everything falls apart.
      i've never been Good at following frameworks,
On another evening, he stares and wonders
      Where my Apathy came from.
I tell him I can no longer use words to love.
He fends for himself inside afternoons now;
In the little windows we used to discover   Together

His day job is nothing if not holding the hand of a woman
    clutching a rosary
It's like he's trying to outweigh
A grief he can't quite grasp.

    He spoke in soliloquies
        inside his eyes: Verses.

We sit in his father's church.
    Why did you turn away? I ask him
Choir men howl until it feels alright again
    I thought I'd never really get rid of you.
He holds my hand.
I squeeze back, as if to say
    You were wrong.
The corners of his lips turn to heaven.
He will never hear me

JANE POIRIER HART

Still Life

When the barkeep replies to my "Roku Negroni, please," with a blank stare,
I curse Yelp. Again. Gin sloshes like water on the shores of Lake Superior.
I feel the person settle on the next stool—all poise and posture.
"I'm Robin. Your name, Red?" That jolt of recognition. "You can call me Mindy,"
I say, quick. No hint of flip. "I'll be Mork, then." We clink drinks. He's wearing
a fitted blazer—vintage, cashmere. My hair, natural then, all autumn curls.
The blazer is robin's-egg blue! For a moment we are a Monet! The paring knife
the barkeep brings to a lime, slips. Puddle of blood and juice. This was all before a tick
took up residence, invited Lyme in, and everything—even my skin—surrendered.

COLLAGE RESPONSE TO RICHARD

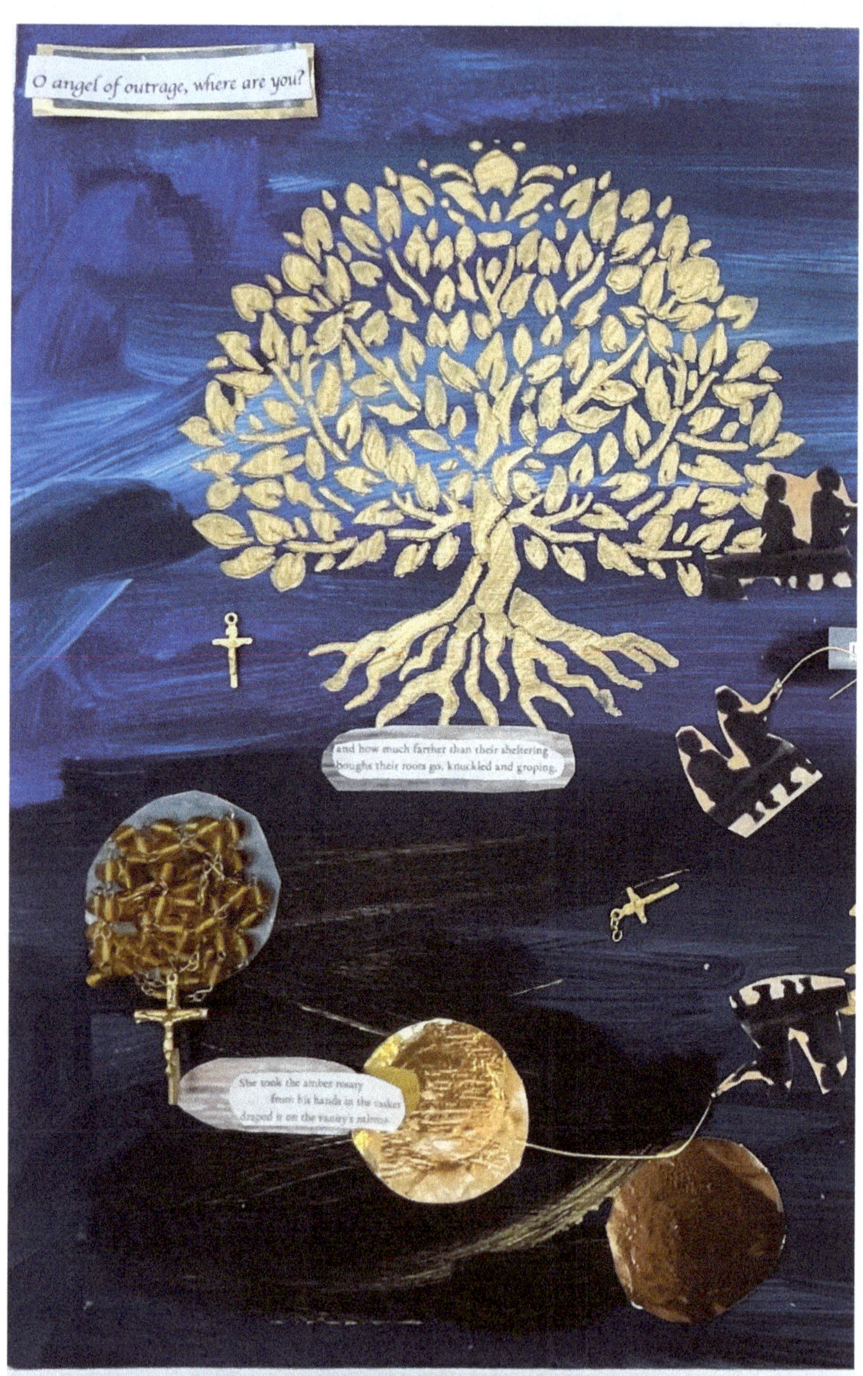

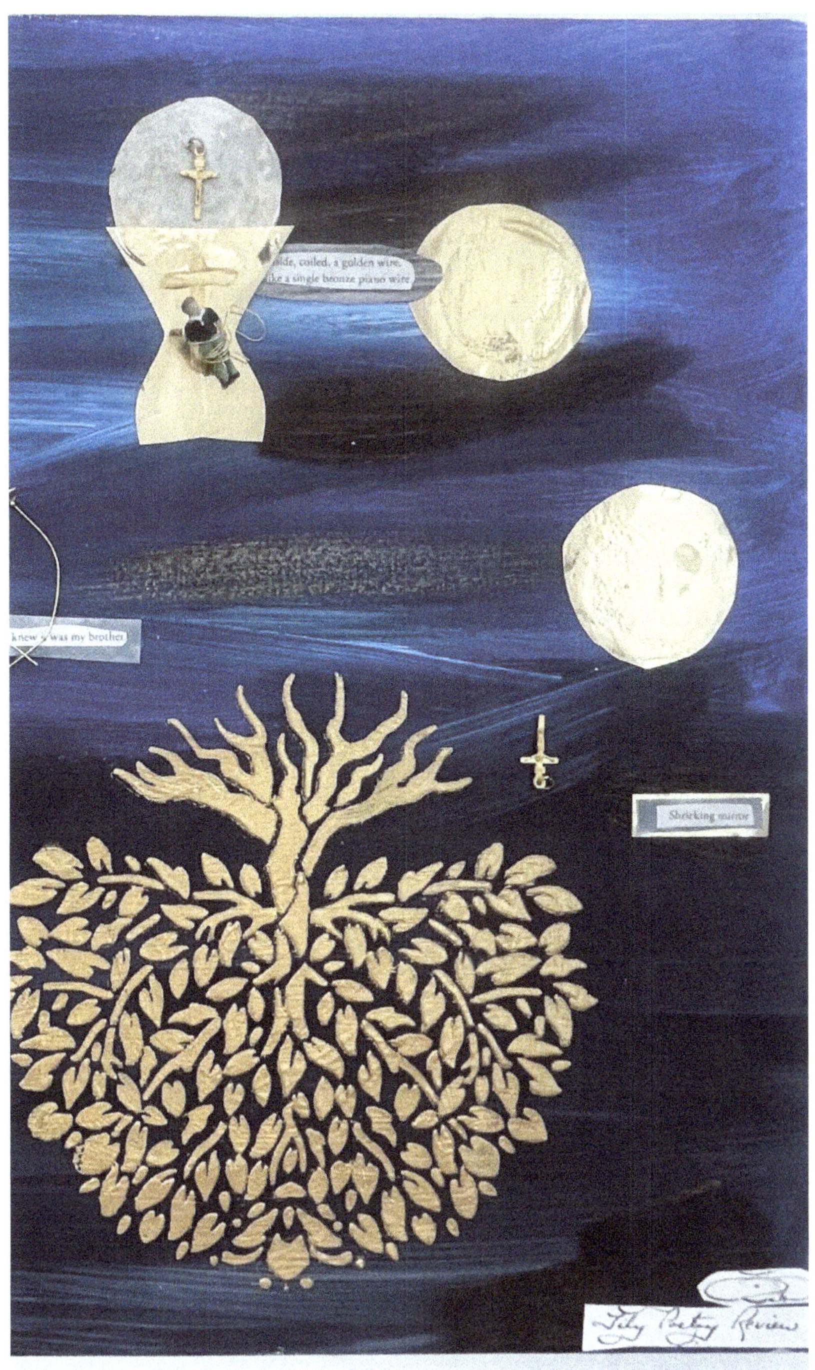
ide, coiled, a golden wire,
ike a single bronze piano wire
knew it was my brother
Shrieking mirror
Tilly Poetry Review

JENNIFER MARTELLI

Key to Collage Response to Richard Hoffman's Poetry Collection, *People Once Real*

All quoted lines are from Hoffman's collection, *People Once Real*. The excerpts are from the following poems (starting from the top left corner, moving clockwise):

1.   "Mundus et Infants"
2.   "Unearthed"
3.   "Betrayal"
4.   "Benedictus"
5.   "The Underworld"
6.   "Unearthed"

Materials:

1.   Acrylic paint on linen
2.   metallic gold paper
3.   gold-tone crucifix and Mary
4.   clay miniature man
5.   gold-tone wire
6.   gold-tone stick pins
7.   amber bead rosary
8.   watercolor on cardstock by Richard Hoffman

CONNEMARA WADSWORTH

Storm's Eye

in this time of drought
a severe weather warning
soil so dry it may float away
            in water's urgent flood,
the storm opens the gun-metal
sky with all its weapons,
rolls and rumbles
            I stagger from my Covid
bed to the roofed porch
a clean break, heat chased,
                    the hay-dry garden may wake
may suckle until the next thirst
now leaves, branches pulled from trees
            are wind-driven across the street
                    in wavelets
            as thwacks of jagged light
crack through clouds
            and needles of rain
                    sing, if the world
            could be washed
clean like this

SONIA GREENFIELD

Behind the door of my office

hangs a Japanese print of a Geisha,
her robes rich with carnation and a riot
of flowers. I remember buying it just
before the city withdrew. In the lower
yellow trim, run through with cherry
blossoms, there is a small irregularity
where I replaced a lost piece with one
made of clay and painted to match
that which was missing. I called a couple
in Manhattan to make sure they were
alive, these old friends I intend to age
adjacent to, and they sent me photos
of the puzzles they were building instead
of going to work on Broadway. I never
thought I'd sit for hours and assemble
such things, but it was all I could do. What
a boon for the jigsaw industry as so many
of us sought comfort in the inane while
our minds tried to assemble a future
that didn't look like that dystopian movie
where all the best characters sacrifice
themselves for humanity. I never thought
I'd glue together puzzles and hang them
on my walls. Jackson Pollock would tell me
such chintz can't compare to action painting,
and of course he's right, though my intention
is the same. I get the picture: headdress
of gold, delicate fan clasped in her left hand,
her obi the blue of a hot, cloudless sky,
but I also see the cracks, the 999 pieces
put together to make an image nearly
whole, and I remember days upon days
at the dining table when spring arrived outside
my windows, and everything bloomed right
on time, while I hid inside and waited
to see who would live or die.

ELIZABETH KUELBS

Hvaldimir

A lone beluga goes rolling through Arctic water
        sporting a harness labeled *Equipment St. Petersburg,*

his home port and pod fogged in the April light
        of Hammerfest, Norway. Straps tight, blubber thin,

he rubs harbored hulls for easement. A fisherman snips
        him free to spyhop among the boats for human touch

and tossed herring, and be named Hvaldimir for whale +
        Vladimir. No one claims him their soldier, spook, deserter,

clown, but he's got craft. He tugs ropes, tangles propellers,
        smiles, whistles, fetches kelp and balls. Naked drunks

dive in with him. Tourists pet his sweet melon, crave pics
        of his viral bubble-blowing body. Not knowing how to

fish, he catches hooks and gashes. Drops weight. But a star
        can't starve, so helpers plump him up until off he follows

catamarans to salmon farms, where he hunts the cod that
        stalk the nets for feed. A one ton pest or pal, depending

on the farmer, they're willing to not kill him,
        and in Hammerfest, there's talk of a fjord where he

and bonded ones like him can scratch their bellies
        on the pebbled bottom. Meanwhile, the US Bureau

of Ocean Energy Management auctions leases to drill
        in Alaska's Cook Inlet.

LINDA ANN STRANG

Aralsk and Izendy,

'We Name the Stars' tells us a circular depression's a crater.
Wencheng, one of the four most beautiful, would have wept,
hands trembling not only over her exile to Tubo. Pale camels

nestle beneath a rusted hull, concentration of pesticides, DDT –
not even a fly would want to live here. But smooth flowed
the Silk Road. Likely the overlords are smooth-talking now –

so long after the leaf-shaped spears, Sogdian inscriptions.
Archeologists were startled by tea buds! So, how many cups
and how many tears to make me an island, poisonous Tengizi?

JULES JACOB

Intersecting Behaviors of Insects & Humans

that which is conquered, conquers at the same time

You study silkworms at thirteen, define metamorphosis
ten years before men, cross the Atlantic at age fifty-
two, Maria Sibylla Marion emerging in Suriname,
cavalier colonizers decimating rainforest like leafcutter
ants, jaws sawing foliage and precious twice stabbed
lady beetles for sugarcane. Copper plates in Amsterdam,
you sketch on vellum. A naturalist assisted by Amerindian
slaves, you note natives save their offspring from bondage
by eating Peacock flower berries to induce abortion.

ELLEN JUNE WRIGHT

I Say Yes

for Angela, enslaved, Jamestown, Virginia, 1619

Am I willing to journey back, close my eyes
and hurl myself backwards in time

live in the incarceration of the plantation,
of *the forced labor camp*

feel the roughhewn floorboards
of the master's house under my bare feet.

Let my imagination be a Time Machine
pulling me back to when it all began,

to when the ship's human remnants
walked on shore, were sold and bought.

Yes, let me be there to meet them.
Let me witness. Let me see their eyes.

DANIEL B. SUMMERHILL

the man at the cafe says to consider the millions who have died for this country & all i can think of is the bullet that struck Ralph Yarl

consider the Black expanse between the mistake

    of property lines & numbers.   consider the wide sky

disrupted by nominalism. every word doesn't make us

    come alive.   consider the hiss brief

artifact forging memory.   i'm told that trauma occurs only

    in retrospect. consider the wound a rupture. consider the bullet

a reentry. consider a boy navigating the myth of america,

    it's lecture of lies.   consider the bullet a mistake

with good insurance.   consider the exit wound: a mothered coffin

consider the exit wound: the legacy

    consider the exit wound.   consider the steep exalt

of a tyrant: a box chevy, a chopping/auction block

    wrap around front porch in Western Missouri where the tulips

grow in reverse—   think of their shape in recollection

    consider the exit wound: a hole too wide to hold

the secret and too american to be of use—

    consider the boy, his salvation,   barely a miracle.

DANIEL B. SUMMERHILL

sitting on a star, thinking how i'm not a star

and it's cold here and the white men up front are playing god again. as we ascend, the air is
convulsing. i learned that during a storm, the plane flies above the fuss. we climb over the sea

somewhere that makes omnificence seem unimaginative, beside me, a man complains about
the lack of meal options to a stewardess who seems unmoved— *what does this altitude know*

of hunger? once, then twice, then every time in TSA, i am selected for "random additional
screening—"   i can't help but pity satan, fallen below this pompous thunder,

named after opposition, checked daily by the mouths of heathens. *where does this rage belong?*
who does it belong to? i'm weary of this posturing vapor, this demi's mischief. bring me exile,

a risen angel in his best bespoke. lightening ray, like an arm reaching up to the heavens pulling
the gods down for baptism. he who has the right to conjure something in his grief. he, whom

which this splitting soil belongs. teach me to be less careful in my rage. learn me the fire.

"sitting on a star, thinking how i'm not a star" borrows its title from Earl Sweatshirt's song,
"Vein"

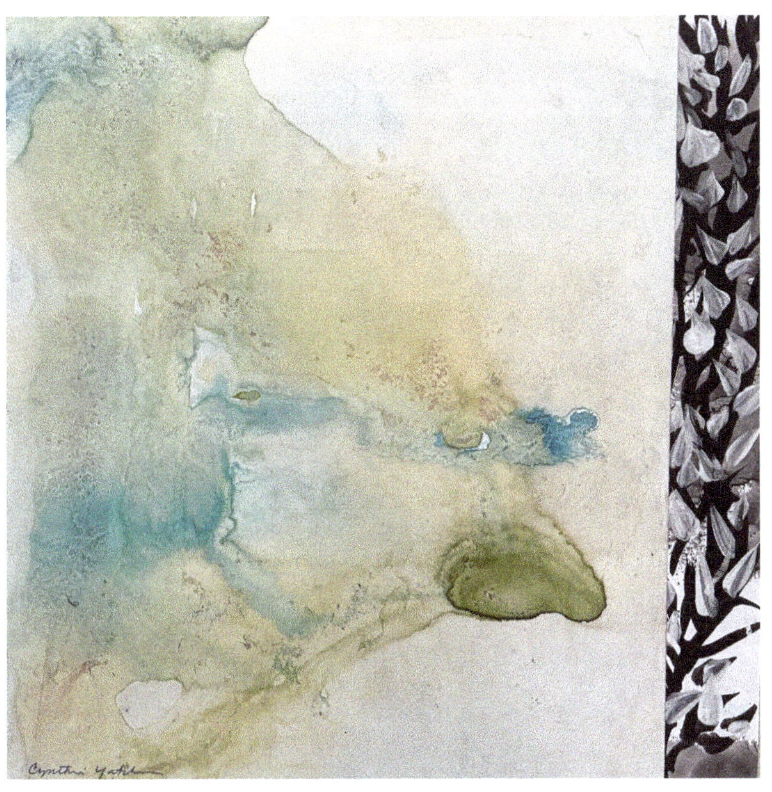

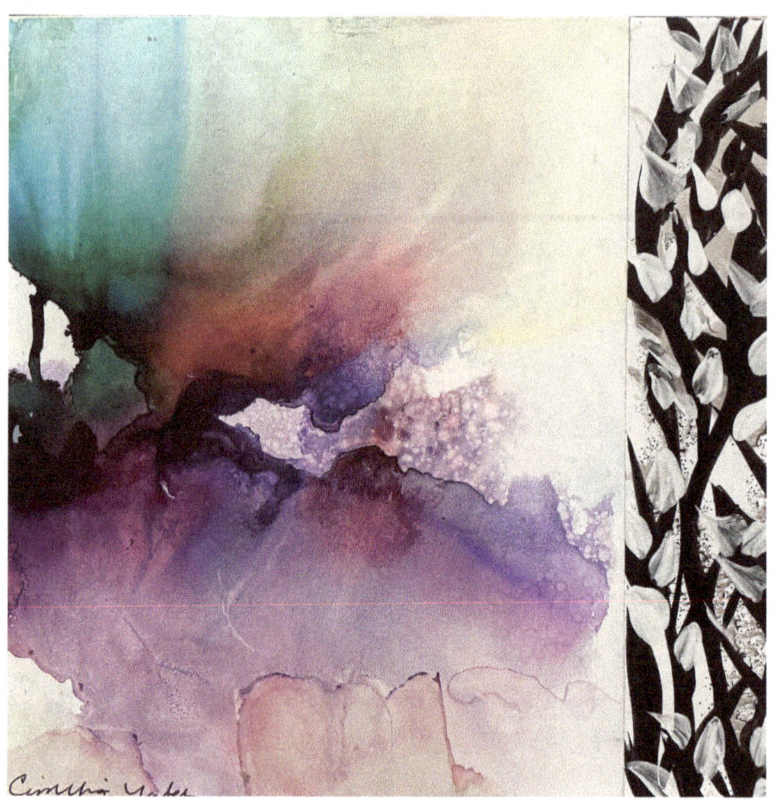

WHEAT

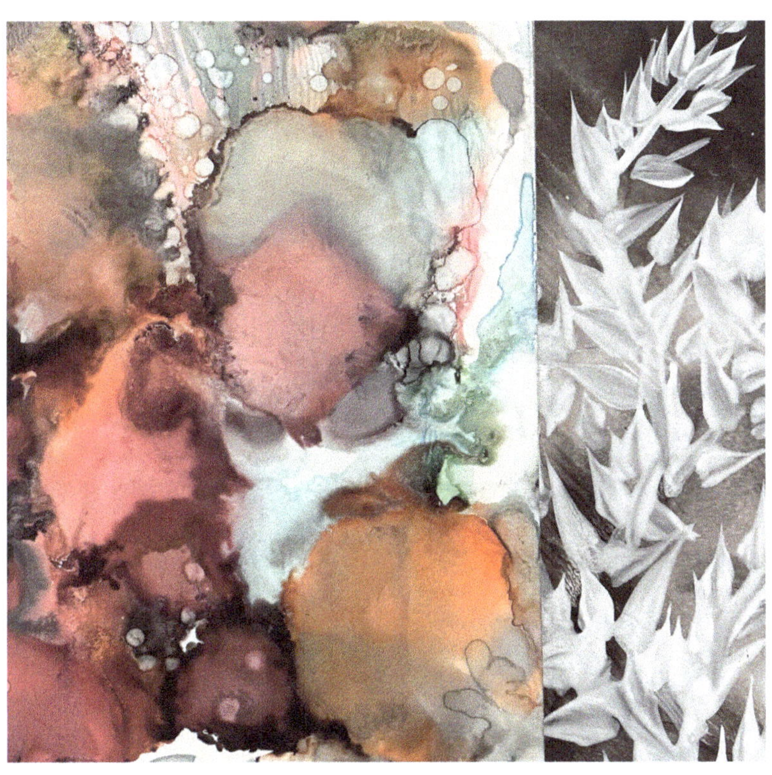

REUBEN JACKSON

Danish Sketches

Copenhagen Sight

Whats it like ?
My Mother asked

When I hail a cab,
They stop-

Words excitedly panted
Across the water

That's all you have
She queried

What else is there
I sighed

II.

Beware pickpockets
The concierge whispered
Chuckling urban child

III.

Restless sunlight
Walking me to the hotel
A 2 AM kiss

IV.

At Ben Webster's Grave (Copenhagen)

Every morning
I walk the tree lined path
To his stone

My questions
An awkward refrain

Were you happier here?
I ask

(Aware that I am projecting
Into sunlit silence)

The cabbie who brought me here
Played an invisible saxophone
The moment I mentioned your name

MARY HUTCHINS HARRIS

If there are no second hands

A violinist's bow will not dismiss the right
cheek first until the Sargasso Sea asks
her to drown in a C minor sieve.

A Katydid will only leap in fear, land
with her parachute wings, to again walk
slowly leaf to leaf, before the next test.

No charmed sheep intestines will be
needed to waltz Hilary Hahn between greens
and blues, even if a whisked wind goes missing.

DANIEL PRITCHARD

Optimism in the End Times

tomato plants inside typhoons
of wire rise with
stubbled vines groping
for richer earth tho
mold daubs the leaves too

a side effect of this
the wettest summer on record

bought in late July on a whim
from a farmer's market
in the parking lot of a clinic
sallow in plastic trays,
they had not yet begun to rot

what fabulist shapes would
their fruit take, bobbling

as hares prance among
the too-low garden boxes
resting in the hedge's shade
not afraid of me or my
neighbors' arguing voices

that crash like sparrows
lost in their own reflection

the circular hush of a plane
gilds the summer air,
muggy with brine and pot
and a gauze of wildfire smoke
under the vermilion sun

what stony haze seems to
grow out of the city itself

like the fur that emerges
from raspberries in the fridge,
bread in the compost,
turning indigestible rinds
into a candyfloss of mold

like the stuffing of a toy
ripped limb and sternum

but then a man whose damp
head is haloed by gnats
whistles as he sheds
his t-shirt, tossing it over
a shoulder, stops and leans

over to the tomatoes
split by the summer profusion

cradles a halfripe pale green
orb on the pads at the tips
of his fingers and takes
the whole of it into his breath,
eyes closed, palm facing heart,

he trots away, almost skips, and
says something about a harvest

DANIEL PRITCHARD

Building 6 Portrait: Interior

—North Adams, August 2016

More typical of student, early or minor phases,
adept at English abbeys, Italian harbors,
at romance landscapes with dim sunsets
behind a cleft of cool-hued mountains,

the world's largest example however depicts
a post-industrial interior, an abandoned
production or storage facility, which could be
a garment factory, but is in fact a portrait

of the gallery space where the massive
painting hangs, a picture of its own absence
in a building the museum absorbed
and memorialized before its renovation,

what was once the Sprague Electric mill.
Watercolor often omits these finer details.
It can be hard to locate a given scene
except through interpretation—en plein air,

white cottons at the beach, dark steam
locomotion, an array of columns—
as without the pertinent details any story
might have been true, or not, which is why,

in its gradations pooling, round at the edges,
stitchworked, dried and layered, transparent,
given to run and bleed, impossible to correct,
in its set, impermeable, flawed, permanence,

a trick that marries time with the stain
that any hand with its light tool can make,
memory is, like watercolor, as the artist said,
the most unforgiving medium.

KAREEM TAYYAR

Reincarnation

in his next life the painter
will turn to the mandolin,

or the starlight,
or the Tarot.

& on nights like this,

with the sky a blank canvas
stretched by the hand of an invisible god,

he will wonder what colors were mixed
to achieve this particular shade that surrounds the moon,

& wonder whether,
for this hour only,

he might ask his former self to return,
if only to answer a question or two.

GRACE MASSEY

Mrs God and Janeway

When I had dinner with Mrs God--or was it Captain Janeway?
we looked out over the Bay of Bengal or possibly Coney Island
remarked on the mantis's smooth strokes swimming in the pepper pot
piloting across the Sea of Tranquility's brothy waves
his breaststroke around the parsnip good god it's a finger
chef's choice, but doesn't God prefer sea bass?
Mrs God genteel, Janeway stoically lost in that imagined universe
lifting a mutual spork of parsnips and fingers
Mrs GodJaneway and me, dining at the Ritz.

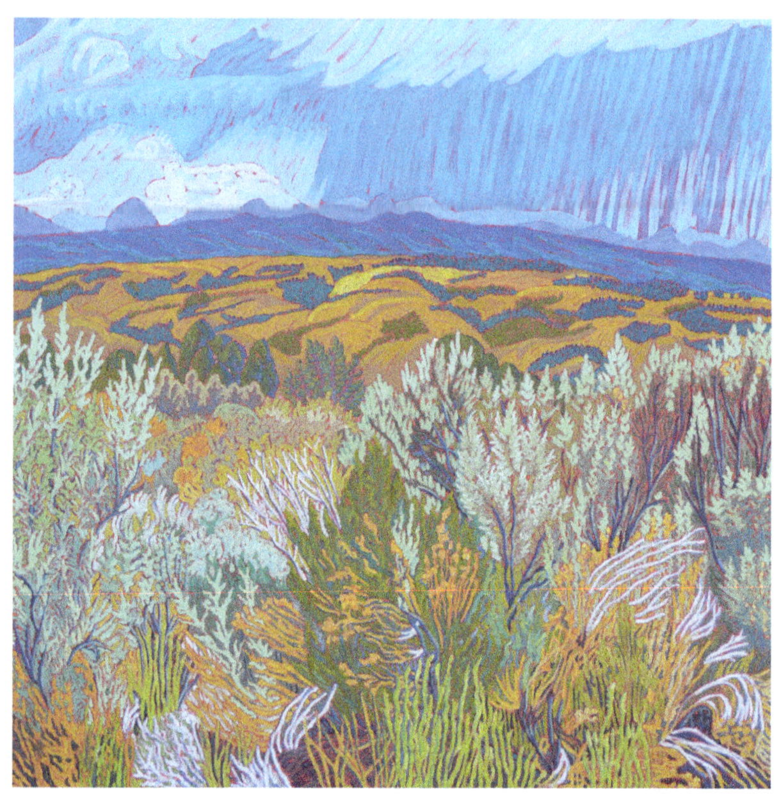

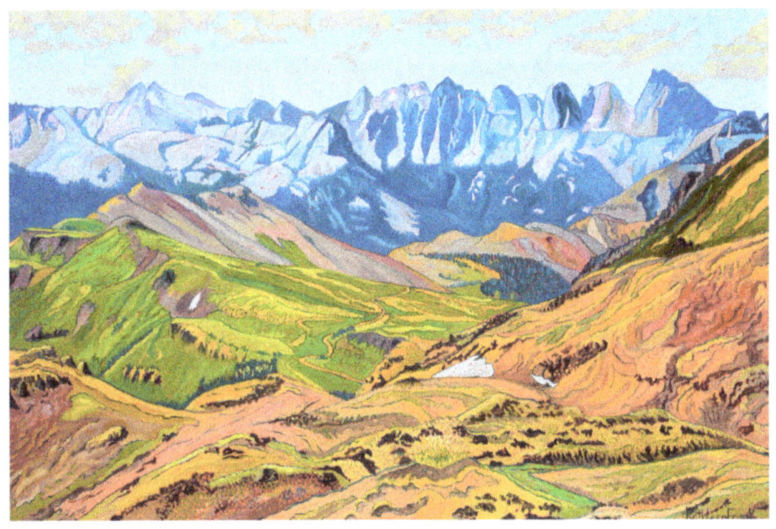

HIKING THE HIGH LONELIES

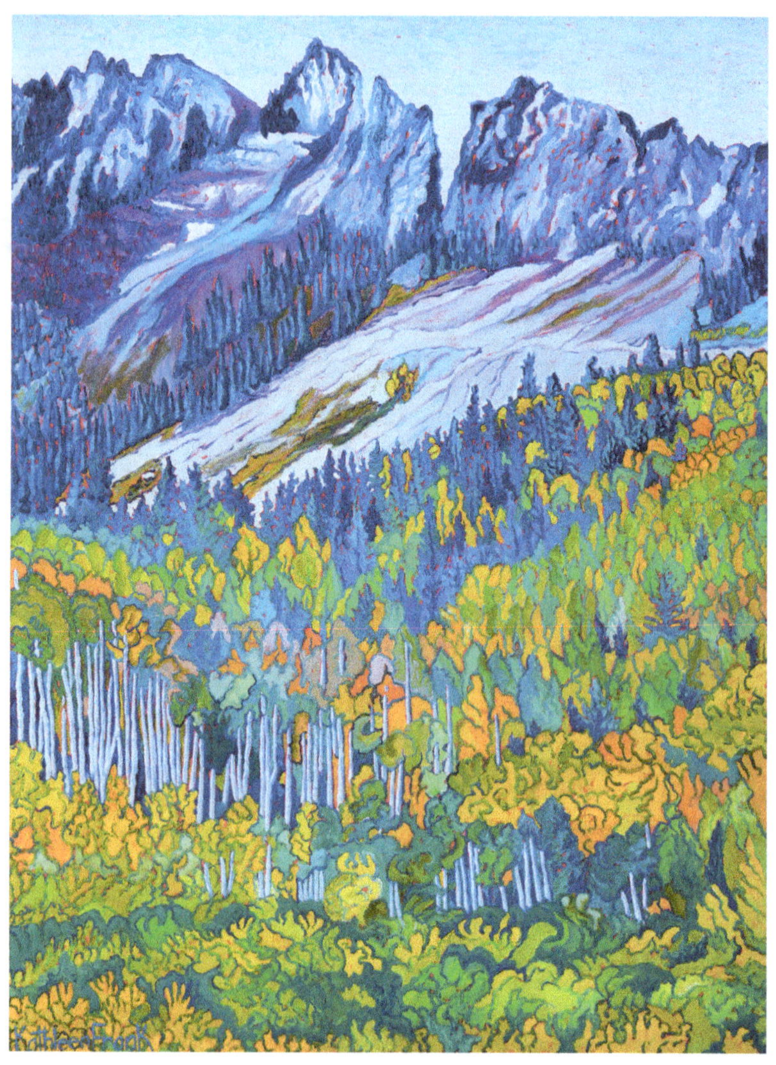

KATHLEEN AGUERO

The Bridge: A Haibun

I cross the Granby Street Bridge in Norfolk, VA, at a moment when
the setting sun and rising moon hang opposite each other. Rush hour,
cars drive by maybe from or toward Newport News where ships in
drydock are raised as high off the sea as the tankers my father worked
on., He was chief engineer repairing what was broken. The gang-
planks were steep and tall with gaps between steps so wide as a child
I feared I might slip through them. When we boarded for sea trials,
I was too frightened to let the captain carry me. I climbed up myself.
My brave mother once let herself be lifted on board in a basket. At
the end of the trial before the tanker headed out to sea, we debarked
mid-ocean down a ladder over the ship's side onto the dinghy waiting
below. I didn't trust the seaman enough to leap into his arms, took
a breath and jumped down on my own. Standing on that bridge,
I study the sun and the moon for a long time before I make myself
trudge back to my boyfriend's house.

Perfectly balanced
Moon and sun are face to face.
I will leave this man.

to stop my body & mind from withdrawing
from known joys

after New England trees shuddered & shed
their last leaves

I thought I had to flee, to cross this country
to desert & days

with piercing blue & burning & walls

thought here
would cure me of there

II.

perhaps I imagined this:
a man as a human life raft
for this life I flung
across 2500 miles

the blurring of cities & bridges
through days of driving
& nights with one eye open
in hotel rooms that reek
of antiseptic dreams

how I disregarded the beauty
of that marvelous journey
by myself, thinking then
that it mattered less

because I was alone

because it was
only me

MARIA LUISA ARROYO CRUZADO

I don't know
how to say "mental illness"
in the Spanish of my family

Abuela's failed cure for bedwetting:
pee on a brick she heated
in the oven, its steam rising up
to exorcise el problema
plaguing me "allá 'bajo"

whenever she saw me reading,
odious fear crawled up in her,
made her spit: ¡Loca!

the same disease, she hisses,
of reading too much lived in her son,
Tío Beto, the one in Puerto Rico

who tried to crush the life & spells
out of her, a malevolent unknown,
sang the murmuring voices, not
the woman who birthed & raised him

Abuela, which spells failed you then?

I still don't know
how to say "mental illness"
in our Spanish

UNTITLED

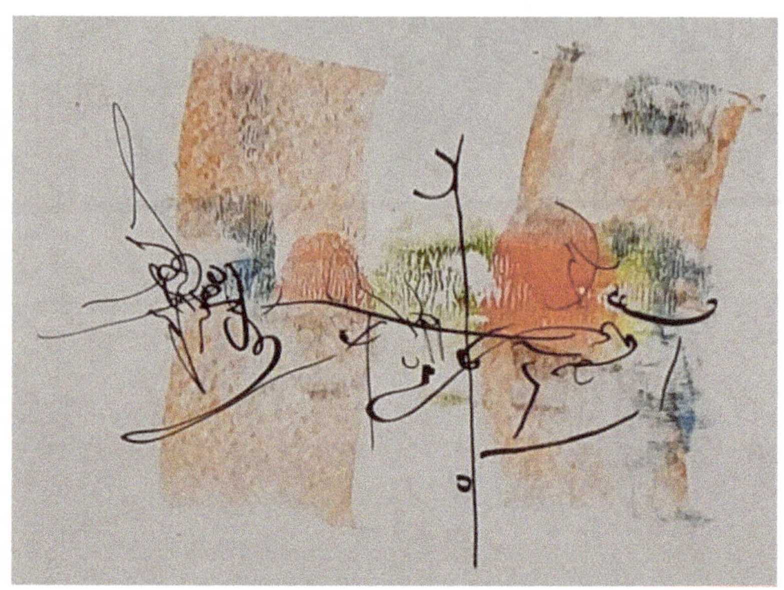

UNTITLED

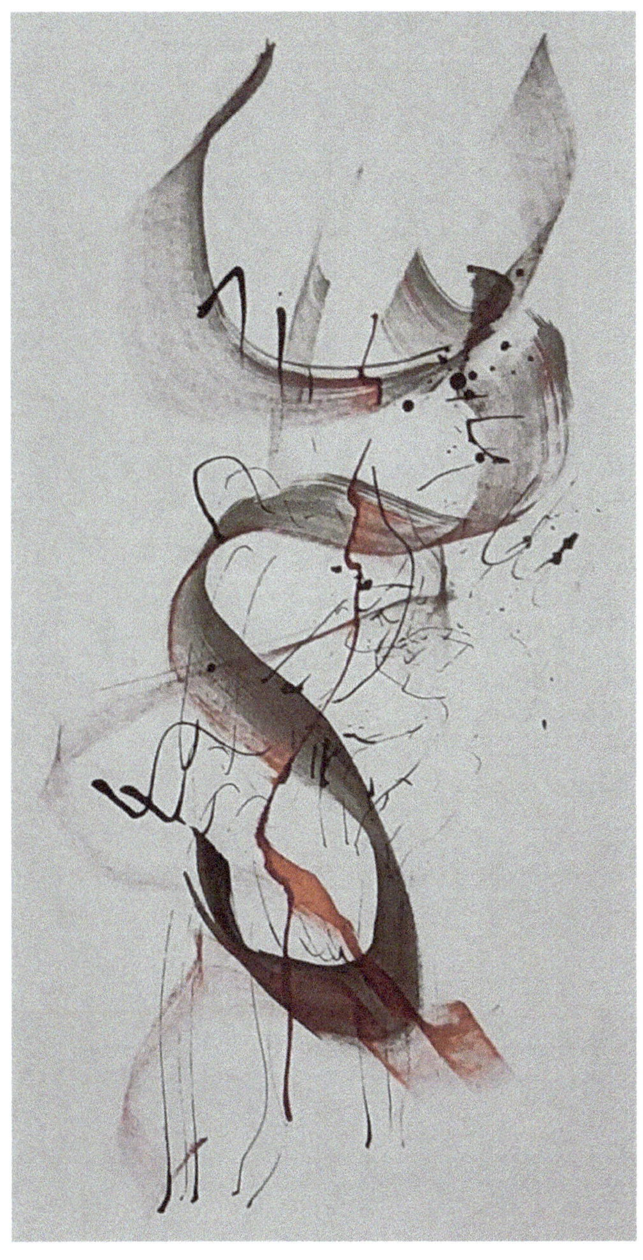

   UNTITLED

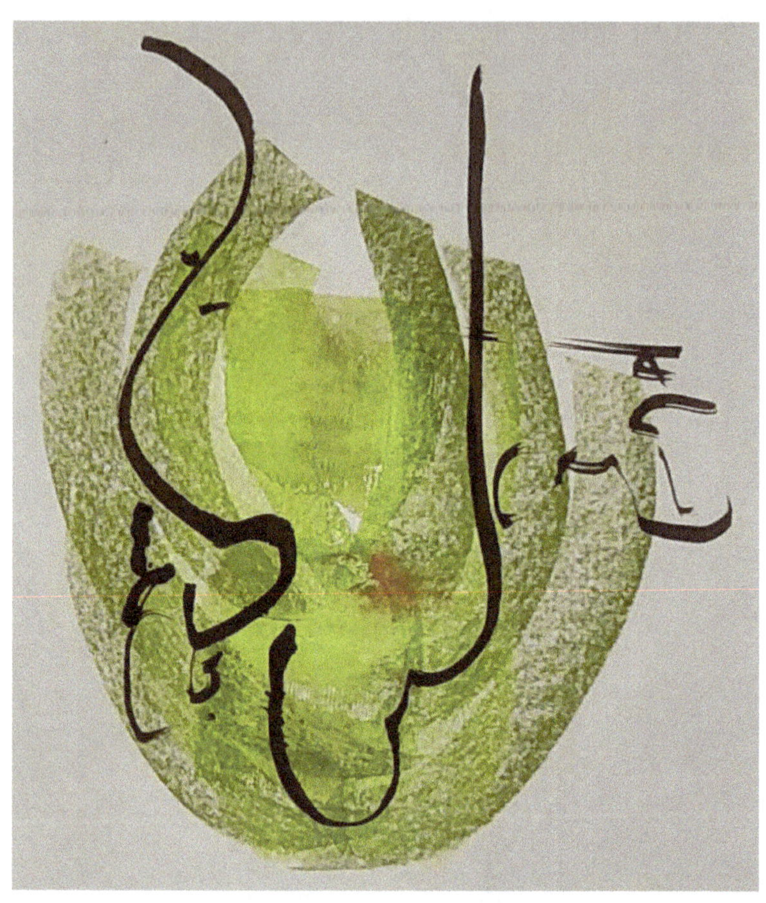

THERESA MONTEIRO

Dear Fernando, March

I want the sharpest ear
existing. Let me hear
the spiders, gothic and good,
hatching beneath
the heaviness of dead
leaves—years of them—
lining the ground of the woods
between us. Amplify the sound
of their fragile legs, while the snail's epoch
unfolds over cold breakfast. The snail
among the leaves with the spiders
leaves his viscous trail
in one direction. You say, *Stop.*
love time, not things. But Fernando,
it's not the same here.
Winters are too much
salt, the history, too short. And hearing
is not doing—but it helps.
Withered hand: save my life.

WYN COOPER

Trailer

Picture so grainy the blue sky's overcast,
tape that holds the signals worn from use.

The production jinxed, the sets
too grandiose for the paltry plot:
Man leaves family to seek work
elsewhere, returns to find family gone.

He wrings his hands, scans
the kitchen ceiling's peeling paint
as if he might find answers there.

A cookie crumbles in his bent fingers.
Crumbs gather on the counter.
In a rage he sweeps them to a floor
so warped by age the blue-eyed marble
his son forgot rolls all the way
to where the wainscot used to be.

The camera pans to pans on the stove
that won't hold heat. His hunger
sends him out for food and drink
but the bar's closed for a wake—
the mourners mourning, the celebrants
roasting the same dead man.
And then the action begins.

ANTHONY WALTON

Freud Invents the Concept of "Cathexis"

He sits deeply in his chair, cradling a cigar, evading her
intensifying need by gazing across the room and into

a glass case full of manuscripts and mementos, calmly –
so calmly – auditing her story. He is without judgment

or inflection: he holds at arm's length the depth of her
suffering, the emotion and tenor – the tremor –of her

voice; still, her language and struggle travel far
beyond the usual clichés of received description

and music hall song that so many of the analysands
summon to envisage and divulge their most intimate

selves. But then he realizes, beyond his well-practiced
detachment, that *his heart is going out to her... -*

yet, as a clinician, as a provocateur, he is aware that such
a simple metaphor is reductive; he must remain within

rigor and distance, while being cruelly accurate. Later,
he will savor working at his desk with a large brandy

and reflection and more tobacco in the coolly dissipating
electrical aftermath of the session. He will make notes.

He will think through how she conveyed her emotions,
the gestures and pained restraint she exhibited. He will

rationalize their interaction, and iterate a human encounter
into scientific knowledge, deflecting any dilation –

compassion, pity, desire – into data and files. He did not,
after all, have feelings. He had, and only, observations.

ANTHONY WALTON

Night Journey, North Of Boston

Drifting what am I like, a gull between earth and sky
Tu Fu said on the road to Tung- t'ing Lake, another road
through time

taking him to a boat that would float him

to an early grave – and I think of winter, summer,
it is always the same, dragging the same heaviness
out of Boston onto the high bridge

over the industrialized mouth of the Charles, drifting
out of my lane and correcting as I reflect upon the way

moments unravel and stay
                                    with you, then ravel

and drift away this late evening as they ride with me
down the far side of the span into Chelsea,
on through Revere, Saugus, and Lynnfield,

an ordinary world that cannot look more strange –

iridescent ribbon of sparkling headlights, sequined
taillights, a wilderness of signs, so much darkness,

so much light – then darkness on 95 up through Essex
County, across the Merrimack, dark

as far as Portsmouth –

the prediction is snowfall tomorrow, four to six
inches –but tonight the quiet sky

is clear and brittle, and I listen to the light wind
rush and envelope the car, while over my head
the stars are in formation: dress blues, parade

rest, each constellated galaxy a gear in the larger
slow clock of the cosmos.

The moon is full,
                but distant.

ii.

Over my head the crab scuttles
through the evening muster,
dimly, but I know it is there: other

stars far and farther,
and Venus, Jupiter,
junk dust, the delicate

lace of our atmosphere,
    spy and telecom

satellites clicking and whirring
all night,
            spinning, stringing

webs, threads of impulse, electricity
and silence. I imagine myself
such an instrument:

lathed and able to see God in the laws of physics,

turned and turning, tuned – or a sextant, anonymous,
fitted to the reach of the void, geared

and grooved into the sky and the way
they both curve

and deepen, past the flat daylight
ceiling and its false promise
of enclosure –

so different from the night blooming
away from me and into itself, out of itself, past the stars
and space junk on the way to becoming
a galaxy –

iii.

There was a time when my hopes were like stars
collapsing and so far from me

they were useless as points of navigation.

There was a time when my perceptions
for stars had something to do with what I described
as the fleshy and blood-filled compass
of my heart,

then that time passed and I learned to stop
making metaphors, to stop dreaming
of one clear light,

cold, brittle and beyond reach –

iv.

The clarity of winter nights, learning to marry
stars with that austerity which is no dream

of spring, I started thinking of cold as sadness
and sadness as the more courageous half

of wisdom, which it is not.

I learned to contentedly walk the snow blown fields
of my own distance, coming upon the lake
ice of my indifference, and came to think of cold
as hunger, a hunger that cannot be fed by stars

or light: we do not die of darkness, we die
of the cold.

v.

Over the Piscataquis River into Maine, the dark
highway through York County like the dark forest
inside me, the startling absence of others
on this road to –

where? – darkness? Bangor?

But this dark is creating a memory

of light, this winter night drifting me to an afternoon
in bright autumn when I stopped on a bridge

in Connecticut, leaves and water rippling below
me, basking sunlight—

and there I was - my reflection—my shadow—
[space]
Nights like this I would be that shadow, spangled
as it was with golden leaves in water

and sun, dark but glittering. In that moment I named
myself *pilgrim*, someone who had traveled
far to a moment when I could comprehend

that my shadow in darkness was the *I* that I
could see, not me most days, most nights,
tonight, someone looking for
Portland, exit 6A –

vi.

*Long wandering will be my fate. I have achieved
nothing, and my tears fall like rain.* Tu Fu died
not on the road, nor drifting
between earth and sky, but on a boat

on the Yang-Tze, drifting, perhaps dreaming
of Li Po, his mentor and friend, on his way
to he knew not where

and I drive on, as if this darkness were an exit,
into myself –

as I must make do with this suddenly new city: over lit,
orange, halogen, and a cluttered night sky –

The two longer quotes in italics are from Tu Fu, translated by David Hinton.

LINDA CARNEY-GOODRICH

Closest to God

Pope John Paul II arrives in Boston in his fancy, roofless car
close to Tinean Beach, where Bulger buries bodies
under the sharp rocks we call, *sand*, where we kids
sweat like dogs, our tongues panting for bomb pops.
His pope-wave renders the crowd silent as church.
The Vicar of Christ is debonair in his white cape and rubied fingers.
As his ride slows, I pray he'll throw us bits of candy and gold.
He meets my stare, his eyes, sapphire knives cutting away all that isn't mine.
I picture my family like ants crushed beneath his wheels.

ANASTASIA VASSOS

Letter to Peter the Priest as He Awaits the Day of Judgment

after Matthew Olzmann

If you see Aunt Helen tell her
I still have the gold hoop earrings.
If you see my parents tell them I'm sorry.
My spine has herniated its disc
and I wake in the middle of the night, askew.
I wear socks to bed.
But why am I telling the dead
something they already know?
Show me the profile of Jesus
on this morning's burnt toast, the Facebook
post of the horse you rode in on
the boat that carried you out.
Show me the coffee grounds at the bottom
of the cup, prophesy my future:
the long journey through the mountains
the stranger I'll meet who'll bestow a gift.
In the Alaskan rain forest
my friend Mistee cared for her dying father
who kept smoking even as he lay
in the unmade bed.
After he died he sent her a crown
of sonnets. I won't ask
if God exists, though I'm curious—
when I pray I'll name you instead—
dear Petros, dear Rock.
Yes. I believe naming is praying.
Though you once said
you are not a man of faith,
I think that was just the blink of your eye—
your hands and heart witnesses

that Christ died for you.
Tell me about the afterlife:
do you still wear the collar? Those shiny clerical robes?
Do you even have a body?
Have you met St. Demetrios?
Find out if St. George is still slaying the dragon, his horse
bucking under him.
Here in Boston winter has slid
into habit, hurling rain and shadow
shadow and rain instead of snow.
The virus lingers, mutates.
I'm left with the lamentation of the sky.
I'm left with two gold coins I forgot
to place on your eyelids when you fled.
Tell me: is there really a river?

STEVEN RIEL
Double Exposure

> *"The Spirit Leaves the Body," photographic sequence by Duane Michals*
> *&*
> *"Leaf Boxes," sculptures by Steve Hollinger*

Young male cadaver in a bare room
on draped daybed or bier.
Window blinds, slightly downcast,
filter sunlight, which wrinkles the wall
into a smoky, ghostly sheet;
sculpts the skin
over his inert ribs; and draws my gaze
towards thick quadriceps. Is this light
clinical, doleful, or both? An hour
could drift by, a dust mote float. What was his
substantial penis rests on one thigh—
object of desire now only a thing.

> Hollow box fashioned
> out of acid-washed leaves.
> Miniature casket of brittle
> membrane held intact
> by a network of veins.
> Coffin tiptoeing on four leggy stems,
> its thin leather lit
> from within. In one corner
> of its cube: tiny crack
> where wraith can waft
> past naked branches.

The deceased's shadow sits up,
swings legs over cotton folds,
walks straight towards me, the specter
of his cock too foggy to ogle.

His outline passes through me
but I feel nothing. It leaves me
with the motionless corpse, an emptier
room. I, too, have a shadow.

A gust shoves a flock of crisp leaves
skittering across the sidewalk just outside.
The eyetooth tip of each leaf's stem,
where it clung to bark,
claws against cement without taking hold.

QUINTIN COLLINS

The End, At Speed

A squirrel flickers from a branch
to the ground, straight to pavement
—probably not the way it planned
to begin the day. Body shut down
or missed step as it bounded
from electric line to tree limb.
These squirrels skitter all morning:
balance and pivot, about face,
jitter along the fence—an energy
devoid of worry as they tweak.
It only makes sense the end arrives
at speed, sky beneath the feet,
ground above the head, body tucked
to reach for the next foothold,
a plummet away from the light.
I perch on the deck. I search
for the squirrel, scan the setback
between my home and the next,
wait for branches and leaves to rustle.
From up on the second floor,
the ground looms nearer than I expected.

Bomb Site

(A departure from Rilke)

Morning ignores it; and who knows?—
the burnt lime trees and pitted block of flats
might be fakes. So might that warm crater

filling with kids—God knows from where—
who play catch with the littlest one's shirt,
then stop to watch a tenant's eldest son

poke under the crushed, incinerated deck,
teasing out twin tea kettles in a washtub.
He looks like he's acting too, for the kids

or anyone naïve enough to think anyone
lived here. Whatever remains is incredible
as history now, where everyone's a stranger.

STEVEN CRAMER

Sisters

(A departure from Rilke)

Notice how they each do the same thing
differently, as if the years between them
made separate spots of time in one room.

Each holds the other, being held. If tired,
one can't wear the other out; and neither
needs to ask if the other one needs blood.

On walks, they used to almost touch, taking
steps that matched, like a march. One died—
what rhymed at one time off-rhymes now.

STEVEN CRAMER

Photograph of Ethan Looking at the Globe, 1999

(A departure from Rilke)

We don't recall if he knew how to spin it.
Afterwards, his profile might have turned
to face us, with his plump look of clarity,

round as a watch, brief as an hour. Now
he barely has time to keep up with time—
what with work, sex, the sleep both require.

Do you, like me, sometimes stop to glimpse
his fingers skimming across the North Atlantic,
as though he had all the time in the world?

  RED BARN

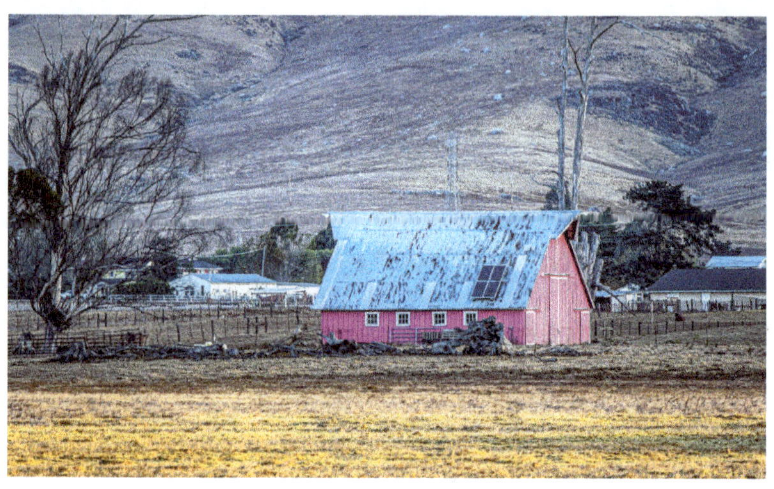

LAURIE FRANCE

TRAPPED LEAF

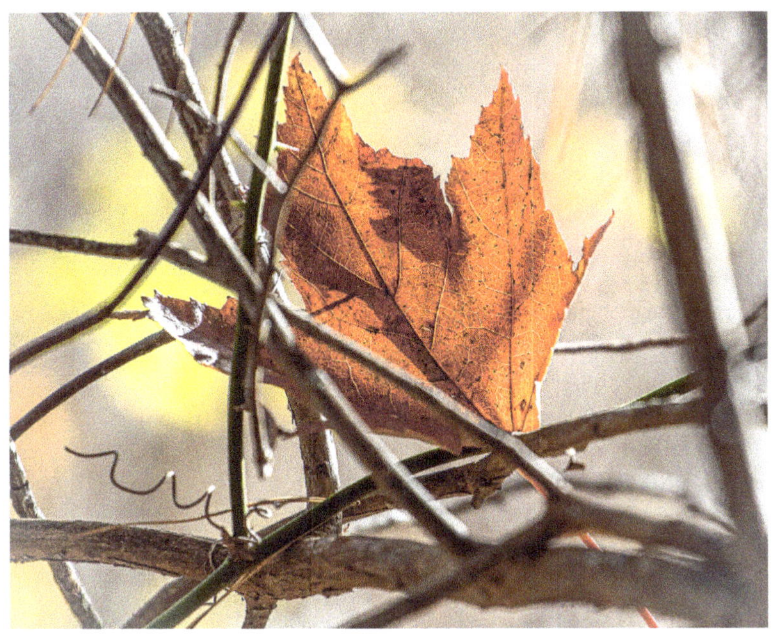

TERRY TROWBRIDGE

Coyote camouflage

A coyote walking his straight stalk
could use the help of corn circle witches
to conceal his pathways of crossed scents
across Niagara's escarpment farms.

One farmer hangs a cornhusk stuffed man
on a tree, in substitute of standing guard herself.
Another farmer hangs a propane tank
from three wooden stakes, with a timer
that lets out sounds like grapeshot.[1]

Between them,
a ditch fills with standing water,
cool at sundown
and just beyond the gaze of migrant workers

who, in the daylight, find only
the footprints of the coyote and
blackish mud smutched with tawny
patches of shed fur.

Dawn, the coyote dips himself
in an irrigation pond
before panting to sleep
with the pack's July dreams
of grown rabbits and overfed mice.

____

1. In the Niagara Region of Canada, these are called "bird bangers."

SUZANNE MERCURY

Moon Rabbit

A change of wind, or did I move

    too suddenly this time—

        a rabbit runs in and then out of sight

into the rain-soaked weeds
                there—

    permanently startled   at the edge

                among many places

The only thing moving between the light

        and the grass—

      It is the light between grass.

Machinery of legs

    soundless, sudden

As when its feet, running   easily turn the earth

        as if to red jasper

      as if to evening, changing its way into black

I want its weight to be enough

    to keep me

on the earth longer

She is the kick:

             amplified

                    into strangeness

Lengthening

                    lengthening as she runs—

SUZANNE MERCURY

Foxes Into Infinity

There, two foxes break into the unripe watermelons in the garden:

       tails high, shredding rind with their feet

           into summer, making fall—

               Redder than the clay from the *Sangre de*
Christo,

          brighter than the sun's nerve net   lit up

in the gold lit evening   that is this undone hour

        a half-shadow   broken, shining and tricking

          the eyes

And I am day-long, bent by everything I once knew

         There they are: glowing and water rusted

       bruised fruit   almost brown

     Wet clay in rivulets, red coals   shuddering to ash in the

      growing downpour.

Here are some instructions for you: stand naked at your window

        watching fox kids devour your sorry garden in
the rain.

If a neighbor going by gives you an odd look,

roar gently at them.

The melons never make it to ripening anyway   I think they are
better

      with fox feet in them like this, fired up and crushed

       against the ground

There they are, again:

        such long legs   folded into infinity

           then leaping after

               this brief rain
ears

                      extended
outward   flickering—

DZVINIA ORLOWSKY

Damaging Wind

Wind hid in the forest. Seasons came and went, but there were
no signs of devastated towns—no boarded restaurant windows or
collapsed porches. No chimes tinkling in the breeze. Some suspected
the wind herself was damaged.

Wind's father had been a boozy hurricane; her mother, a heated
argument between lovers in a cold motel room. But what was her
calling card? An overturned flowerpot, a torn kite lying in tall grass,
pages rustling in an open, unread book?----Occasionally a shingle
flapped on a neglected barn roof, or a heavy damp branch dropped
on a neighbor plucking lawn mushroom after days of rain. But no one
stood outside and said *the wind is going to be nasty tonight.* No one replied
tell it to the wind.

***

Nearly forgotten, Wind considered staging a comeback. She could
ruin a birthday party with flying debris or chase off the clowns who
were trying to take over the neighborhood. She could even make
them tumble. She could slap power lines onto asphalt roads, though
pushing a car off the road often left her gasping.

Hoping to gain more visibility, she tweeted a picture of herself as
a fully erect windsock. This got her three followers. *You're the butt of
all jokes*, the leaves rustled. *You're just a flash of color*, Wind muttered
defensively. *Then a crumbled bit of nothing.*

Shamed, Wind mimicked dog whistles. Silenced, she became a shot of
rum, a blown over kiss, a mouth puckered in the hot, still air.

AMANDA SHAW

***Previously Owned* By Nathan McClain**
Four Way Books, 2022

Nathan McClain's meditative and elegant second book, *Previously Owned*, investigates the self in its physical and psychological locations. The book's introspective intensity reveals a generous writer willing to share his deep engagement with the audience in whatever he encounters.

McClain's speaker is in constant dialogue with himself, with art and history, landscape, race and the American justice system—and with love in its many forms. The book begins with a meditation on *Boy Pulling a Thorn from His Foot,* the ancient Roman statue known as "Spinario." The speaker, standing in the darkening museum, searching for some understanding of pain, addresses himself directly (and not without irony) as "you… / with your notepad and pen." From the outset, he notes the tension in the boy's posture—

> bronze body curled into
> question
>
> mark, not pulling,
> rather, about to pull
> the thorn, finally, out.

This liminality—something about to happen, but never to happen— is evoked in the paradox McClain later uses to describe the thorn as "thrumming / still," capturing sculpture's ability to hold motion in stillness. As the poem winds down, subject and object begin to merge: just as the boy seems "so close" to removing the thorn, the speaker is admonished to "Step back" by a guard:

> […] his one job
> to enforce the distance
>
> necessary, which might be called
> perspective, though
> not yet.

As is true throughout *Previously Owned*, the denotation/connotations of words and phrases are used elegantly here. "Perspective" means several things at once: the technique in art ("discovered" long after the Spinario); the different angles from which guard and speaker see the statue; and the "necessary distance" any artist needs to render painful experience into art.

In later poems, McClain gestures skillfully at the conventions of the pastoral, aubade, and nocturne. He draws on form—particularly repeating lines, words, and patterns—to produce tensile, uneasily balanced poems. The villanelle "Sisyphus: To Do List," for example, uses the repeating line and end-rhyme structure to convey the mythological character's cycle of absurdly mundane but never-ending obligation. The uneasy symmetry of these poems gives the impression of menace held at bay through delicately crafted structures—they are, like the thorn, thrumming *and* still.

In several poems from the first section, childhood landscapes and experiences with reading complicate the speaker's struggle to overcome alienation from his new life in the New England countryside. The long poem "Where the View Was Clearer" is narrated by an older self confronting a rural setting he has only encountered in books—a place where he should feel secure, given "a job [...] with excellent dental." The beauty and *almost*-familiarity of the present landscape alternate with a memory from Southern California of climbing rocks, terrified of a stepfather who would "kill him" (ostensibly for leaving his younger brother behind). Something in both landscapes calls to him, but in each he is alone. The abundance of pine, spruce, organic corn and jacks-in-the-pulpit is compelling, but its strangeness makes his mind "impenetrable"—

My wife asked,

What are you thinking?
or *What's the matter?* but

I was a stand of trees by then.

He ends the poem with a (perhaps) more successful attempt at communication:

> I wish
> you could have seen it, I said.
>
> You'd have hardly believed—
> A family of rams, I swear.

The aside "I swear" typifies McClain's style—so characteristic of Elizabeth Bishop, who is directly alluded to—indicating that his attempts at communion are earnest but provisional, at least for now. Time and again the speaker of these poems questions himself and revises truths expressed in previous lines, somehow never appearing uncertain despite avoiding all proclamation.

The majority of section 2 is a series of minimally punctuated poems beginning with the line "They said I was an alternate." In a note, McClain explains that he wrote these after being selected for jury duty, where his position as an alternate meant he was forced to watch an entire trial but remain silent as another black man's fate was decided. The poems are short and convey the contradictions inherent in his position, with play on the meaning of the word "sentence" and effective use of phrases like "Can I get a witness." It's impossible to give a sense of the power these poems have as they accumulate, but McClain again captures the irony of his position through form: the ambiguity of the punctuation and lineation contrasts with the foregone conclusion of the "sentence." Techniques like varied stanza length and the skillful re-arrangement of space on the page help us to reconsider recurring themes and concerns.

In the third section, like the first, contains love poems—my favorite, perhaps, is a fanciful Romeo and Juliet set in a Home Depot—and poems that engage overtly with race and American history. One of the book's epigraphs, "If you start your history with slavery, everything then seems like progress," is explored in all its ironies in the poems that appear here. The section begins with a poem ostensibly written about *Die Hard* character Al Powell, but referring specifically to Tamir Rice ("toy gun… / I didn't know…") and, more generally, to story after story of black men and boys murdered by police—

> And the boy
> had no name

you could sew
into a tee shirt,

minor character that he was,
Powell too,

who, I should probably add,
was black

…though what

else did I expect,
what had I paid

to see in this dark
that I hadn't already seen.

In "Multiple Choice," McClain uses the memory of a used ("previously owned") American history textbook to undermine "answers […] simple and dependable" with which to fill in literal blanks on school tests. McClain's references to race come also in subtle wordplay:

> I sat at a distance
> that softened the edges of white chalk
> on the board (poor vision) though even
> that didn't make me much care to commit
>
> the past to memory except to darken
> the right bubble on the test sheet—

Ultimately, he places his own potential story directly into one of these blanks:

> Until ______________, years before
> I met my wife, I could have been
>
> dragged off for simply glancing at her—
> which I do often…

"Textbook" examples of horror—Emmitt Till and countless other lynchings—are never far. Still, the speaker finds solace in current freedoms, "shelves lined with the past / and its usual despairs. Its joys as well." Above all, he cherishes the agency that love and quiet domesticity can provide:

> A cat, on the windowsill, asleep.
> My wife in a rocking chair. Quietly
> reading. Everyone keeps asking when
> we will finally have a baby,
>
> because it's a thing we can choose
> now. I mean how lucky is that?

I have no doubt that if I began to write about any one of the poems in *Previously Owned*, I would discover the genius of its craft—but the grace and humility of voice that characterizes all of the poems is the book's most salient characteristic.

A good friend of mine who is not a poet wrote

> The little contemporary poetry I've read seems to try for unexpected associations and connections for the sake of sounding smart or witty or fresh. I feel no sense of pretension reading McClain. In every poem, there's authenticity, earnestness, and fierce intelligence. He approaches love, time, art, and race with the same sure and honest voice— his mind is the constant.

I would add that the messy process of thought and the contingent nature of any experience are never absent from the poet's consciousness. Like my friend, I often felt as if he were sharing his work (and self) with a respected, even beloved confidant. McClain has written a gorgeous book: how lucky we are to be able to read it.

GORDON KIPPOLA

Visiting Her in Queens Is More Enlightening than a Month in a Monastery in Tibet By Michael Mark
Rattle, 2022

> and she spoke a strange language and / left and came back
> without a son and / left and came back and never came back
> ("Portrait in Alzheimer's Disease")

Visiting Her in Queens Is More Enlightening than a Month in a Monastery in Tibet won the 2022 Rattle Chapbook Prize, a prestigious annual contest attracting several thousand entries, out of which only three manuscripts were selected for publication. In addition to a copy being mailed to more than eight thousand *Rattle* subscribers (an enormous print run for any writer's first book of poetry), Michael Mark's chapbook earned the distinction of becoming the journal's all-time best seller online, according to *Rattle* editor Timothy Green. "We also had many subscribers ordering extra copies for friends and family," Green said, "I think it's both because Michael is a brilliant poet of empathy, and also because so many people are going through the experience of helping their parents through the end right now."

The book's front cover photo, overlaid by one of the longest titles in literary history, is of a woman nearing her nineties, sipping coffee by a window through which nothing is visible, in a room with a faded decor that passed from modest fashionability at least fifty years ago. This woman's name is Estelle, and we don't know it yet, but soon, regardless of warts, frustrations, and tragedies, we'll learn to value, mourn, and cherish her as if she were our own mother, our own grandmother. Turn the book over, here's Estelle's sixty-something son, the poet Michael Mark, standing in the same space, now emptied. The stories and the emotional resonance of these two images, connected on a single sheet of 9" x 12" cardstock, separated by time and death, is a bonus visual poem: a sonnet expressed in photographs.

The finely crafted free verse poems comprise two dozen absorbing family photos brought to life: as if they were scenes from a play we're watching from the wings of an intimate theater; as if they were conversations we're overhearing through the thin walls of our adjoining apartment; as if we've been invited inside to sit on a worn, sagging brown couch. Michael Mark's book is an unflinchingly honest, devastating, and celebratory exploration of the poet's relationship with his parents, of shifting family dynamics during the Alzheimer's disease afflicted final years of his mother's life, and of his relationship with a now ninety-seven-year-old cantankerously persevering father.

Alzheimer's disease is the most common form of dementia, a progressive memory and cognitive function disorder that currently afflicts at least six million Americans, mostly sixty-five and older. Most families know, or will eventually know, the sadness and trauma of experiencing the essence of a loved one slipping away: a grandparent, a parent, a spouse. In my mid-sixties, and at least partially aware of how many steps I've lost, the specter of Alzheimer's terrifies me. An accumulating joy and comfort of this book is witnessing the adult child's acceptance of his mother as her disease transforms her into … not the same mother he's known, exactly … but a person still worthy of respect and love.

Mark is a poet of observation. "What did you eat today, Mom? / She says tuna. // the correct answer is crust from a lemon / pound cake she shredded with her chewed fingers / then puzzled together." ("Sparrow"). A compelling specificity might be the only legitimate path to the universal: a proposition well-proven in Mark's poems. One of many examples, from "Losing My Parents in a Small CVS Drug Store": "The stock boy caught them in the Employees Only restroom, admiring / the hand soap and the bathroom spray, Hawaiian Calm."

In "Spoiled," Mark enacts the protective stoicism of precise numbers, employing a stanza of end-stopped lines in a poem otherwise liberal with enjambments (some jarring us into disassociation):

> I do the math: she has been gone exactly seventy-three hours.
> The stamp on the carton warns the milk expired five days ago.
> The pulmonologist alerted me it was *a matter of hours*.
> They were married two months shy of sixty-five years.

Along the book's path, we encounter many opportunities for smiles, for surprises of outright laughter. From "She Fools Me Every Time":

> When she soils herself and asks
> if she smells, I take a big whiff, say, *No.*
> Do I?

From "Nothing's as Hard as We Make It":

> Get out from under my feet, I tell her—
> like she'd told me countless times. Go
> have fun with the other dead moms.

Open the book to the middle: here's another visual poem, facing-page photographs of Estelle and Bob caught in a moment of shared joy during their seventh decade of marriage. From "Estelle and Bob":

> My father kneels at my mother's grave
> to ask her permission to go on match.com.

In our "real world," a world we leave behind in the enhanced and often truer reality of a Michael Mark poem, ninety-something Bob probably didn't print out pages of dating site profiles to read aloud to his recently deceased wife. He surely didn't move on via a "meet-cute" parking lot fender-bender as described in "First Date." Mark's poems strike us as authentic personal history, as family anecdotes flavored with the hyperbolic flourishes we accept (and expect, enjoy, and demand) from our most entertaining storytellers. The scenes he presents can move, at times, from dramedy into pure fantasy. In "Souvenirs," the speaker's mother is gathering up "freebies" prior to departing a hotel room (and who among us hasn't slipped a tiny bottle of shampoo into a bag to take home?). Along with the box of tissues, the hangers, and the coffee maker, "She takes the Atlantic Ocean, folds / it over several times to fit // into my suitcase." On some level, this miracle becomes believable: though still alive, Estelle has already ascended into the realm of myth. No reasonable person doubts the abilities of the gods, just as no child doubts their parents can do magic. The final stanza of "Estelle and Bob" also didn't happen. At the same time, it absolutely did happen, and I'll fight anyone saying otherwise:

> He pulls some short weeds, places three pebbles
> on the craggy head of the stone, and sings
> Happy Birthday, raising his voice at her name,
> so everyone knows he's with her.

Approaching the book's end, here's one more poem-via-photograph to savor: two spoons, the left slightly smaller and somewhat differently shaped than the right, both scratched and pitted from decades of daily meals and washings. The handle of the left-hand spoon is engraved with the corporate font of *HORN & HARDART CO.*, a food services company that opened its first New York City automat restaurant in 1912. Very popular during the Great Depression, the chain began to decline in the 1960's, its final restaurant closing in 1991. The handle of the right-hand spoon more specifically reveals how this cutlery entered a lifetime of service in Estelle and Bob's apartment: *PROPERTY OF HORN & HARDART CO.*

"A Daily Practice," the book's final poem, is somewhat of a departure. Estelle and Bob aren't present, but their spirits shine through in lessons their son learned through participating in their lives. The poem's speaker writes the word *Temporary* on red, yellow, and green sticky notes, pressing them first to "socks, silverware, bills, my hair," then to the maple trees in his yard, to his car, to his house—to fear, to hate. This poem is informed by Michael Mark's years as a hospice volunteer, and by a Buddhist practice begun in middle-age. Wisdom brings the realization that nothing is permanent, not our relationships with the people we love, not even the sticky notes or the word *temporary*—"sometimes a wind / comes. And I stumble around, trying to catch them."

A reviewer's eternal limitation is that no description, analysis, or critique of any tangible artistic creation can measure up to the thing itself: sculpture, painting, song, movie, poem. I'll type out page 35 of Michael Mark's chapbook and let it speak what it is, let it tell you what it sees: on its own terms, in its own beauty, and with its own strength.

Celebrating His 92nd Birthday
the Year His Wife Dies

He goes to Ben's Deli
because the waitress doesn't ask how he is.
He takes most of the corned beef
from the sandwich, piles
it on the edge of the plate, makes
a thinner one, with enough left for two
nice ones at home.

The waitress packs his leftovers, extra
slices of rye and half sour pickles
in wax paper and two mustards in squat cups.
She never removes the other setting.
She lets him sit as long as he wants.

To enjoy more of Michael Mark's poetry, visit michaeljmark.com.
Copies of *Visiting Her in Queens Is More Enlightening than a Month in a Monastery in Tibet* may also be purchased there through a link to rattle.
com.

KAREN HILDEBRAND

This Strange Garment By Nicole Callihan
Terrapin Books, 2023

In fall of 2020, during the darkest days of pre-vaccine pandemic, just as we were facing a nerve-wracking presidential election, Nicole Callihan was diagnosed with breast cancer. She wrote the poems of *This Strange Garment* as she went through multiple surgeries and radiation treatment, and on into her recovery. Callihan has been forthcoming in interviews about the circumstances of her medical treatment, yet her poems largely skip the logistics. While the poems themselves slide such concerns into a drawer along with the bills and unfathomable insurance paperwork, we can't help but read between the lines to imagine the daily disruption caused by such a medical crisis. The poems possess an immediate urgency about life, asserting that yes, it must proceed, in all its harrowing gorgeousness.

This Strange Garment worked on me like a concertina, the accordion-like musical instrument with bellows that expand and contract. Callihan's strongest poems are composed with conversational, long lines full of rumination, expressed in a voice as close and intimate as journal entries or late night conversations on the porch with your oldest friend. These are the expanding concertina bellows. But as the concertina must also contract in order to continue making music, Callihan alternates these poems with lyrics of compressed language and shorter lines. In the lyrics, the prominent "I" recedes and meaning slips behind the veil of metaphor. It's a nice change of pace. Not that the poet ever spares us the intensity of her situation. Rather, these lyric interludes allow us to observe from a greater distance. They give us time to catch our breath—like the lungs of a concertina.

The book's opening poem, "Everything is Temporary," is a good example of the ruminative expansive style. It's a three and a half page prose poem that preserves the use of the poetic line. Callahan gives each sentence its own line with a full stop and a double space between to allow for a breath after each statement. She places the speaker in two physical settings, using them as a platform to tell us what she's thinking. First there is an **MRI** test in process; then, the train ride home. "If I were faceup in the MRI machine, I'd see the cherry blossoms are affixed to the ceiling. // But I'm facedown. // My arms extended above my head." From there, she breaks away immediately to consider the aerodynamics of a crane: "A crane, I read this morning, can stay aloft for up to ten hours. // It barely needs to flap its wings." The leap allows us to understand the discomfort of the MRI machine by conjuring a figurative desire for escape. Then, she launches into repetition, a signature aspect of the poem:

> If I'm scared, I should squeeze the egg.
>
> I'm scared, but I don't squeeze the egg.
>
> *Everything is temporary*, I say in my head.
>
> *Everything is temporary*, I say over and over.
>
> This makes me feel better.
>
> *Everything is temporary.*
>
> Until it makes me feel worse.
>
> *Everything is temporary.*
>
> But feeling worse feels foolish, because really, *Everything is
>   temporary.*

The repetition of "everything is temporary" allows the phrase to subtly shift in meaning. Not until midway through the second page is the reason for the MRI revealed, in a conversation with a woman on the train ride home—the second physical setting of the poem:

> *I have breast cancer,* I say, *and really don't want to deal with
>   Covid during my surgery*
>
> *Everything is temporary.*

The speaker inhabits the train location for a mere four lines, before she leaps back to the cranes, where the words "monogamous" and "mating" suggest fertility and anxiety about the impact of this medical situation on her marriage—

Cranes are perennially monogamous.

I'm not sure what this means, but Wikipedia tells me it's
important, that scientists study it.

If early mating attempts fail, they will divorce.

Everything is temporary.

I suppose a failure for cranes is simply something that doesn't
result in an egg, which won't result in a bird, which won't result
in 20-30 years of flight.

In the poem's final stanzas are details of time the poet has withheld
up to this point: "Today is the thirteenth anniversary of my wedding;
it is the seventh month of the pandemic; it has been three and a half
weeks since I found out I have cancer; the election is in fourteen days."
She then leaves us with images of the clouds and river outside the
train window—all figurative ways to say, yet again, "everything is
temporary." The train, the river and even the clouds are in motion,
mirroring the speaker's movement through her circumstances and
emotions. In this way she allows her readers to come along with her on
the book's journey as it unfolds.

Two favorite examples of Callihan's lyric poems are "The skin, right
now" and "Cavity," that appear in the last half of the book. "The skin,
right now" is a sonnet whose title is an extra line. The poem's extended
metaphor of an eraser becomes yet another iteration of "everything is
temporary":

someone might write their name
in pencil; drag their hand
along the graphite; wipe the smudge
on their jeans; decide against it;
take the pink pearl from its pouch;
and rub so hard at the letters
as to make a hole;

The poem's only punctuation is a series of semicolons that separate phrases and form one long sentence—as if to say a life with cancer is a long sentence, or maybe to comment on the lengthy list of post-surgical instructions. The semicolons are a heavy, formal choice of punctuation—one way to suggest burden. This poem ends section III of the book, a section that enumerates side effects along with other surprising events such as a relocated belly button: early onset of menopause, sleep deprivation, aching joints.

"Cavity," in thirteen left-justified lines, appears early in the following section IV:

> One of the places to carry grief is in the mouth.
> A recess, tongued hole, memory of the eaten.
> To be filled with composite, metal, ceramic.
> Not to be held as a memorized passage is held.
> Or a lie. Your tongue. A drink. Crushed petals.
> A title. Victor. Sinner. Wife. A title modified;
> Proud victor. Reluctant sinner. Obedient wife.

The poem lets the empty space of a decayed tooth stand in for surgically removed body parts, perhaps tumors as well. Midway, the poem offers a list of titles—Victor, Sinner, Wife—then modifies those titles, suggesting that the speaker has been modified, by surgery and the experience of a life-threatening illness.

Though these shorter-lined poems shift the pacing of the book—allowing us, like the concertina, to breathe—they don't alleviate the intensity, but allow us to take a step back and observe things from a safer distance. In poem after poem of *This Strange Garment*, Callihan persists with unflinching perceptions of this horrifying and breathtaking, highly personal experience. Despite what is at risk, this book is full of hope. A good example is "The Pain Scale," one of the few poems in which Callihan gives us some hard medical evidence straight up:

> despair, be in disrepair, what's the difference,
> I asked, between pain and discomfort,
>
> am I feeling pain that you've cut off my breasts,
> that you've slit me from hip bone to hip bone

and taken skin and fat from my abdomen,
taken the tiniest blood vessels and moved them

to make these sort of breast-looking breasts, …

Still, she ends the poem with heart-swelling vulnerability:

between a five and a six, I think, but maybe
a two or so, maybe an eight, but god, I'm ready

for a pleasure scale, and not moderate pleasure, I want
severe. Severed but raptured. Not comfort but pleasure.

Pure unadulterated pleasure. *Ten*, I want to say, *ten*.

KRISTEN HEWITT

West: A Translation By Paisley Rekdal
Copper Canyon 2023

"What if the point of grief is not its resolution but the extension of memory, the insistence that the listener, too, carry our history into the future?" Paisley Rekdal's latest collection, *West: A Translation*, asks us to do just that. A hybrid work of poetry, essay, documentary, and archival materials, *West* chronicles the completion of the transcontinental railroad and the Chinese workers who emigrated to the United States to build it. The book takes on the monumental task of elegizing those workers, in the process deepening our understanding of the history of the US railroad and subsequent Chinese Exclusion Act—and connects this history to anti-Asian violence in the present day.

During construction driven by American Western expansion and "manifest destiny," Chinese workers were heavily recruited from China for cheap labor, only to suffer from racist exploitation. On *West*'s accompanying website, Rekdal writes "No one knows how many Chinese workers died during the railroad's construction"; though some ten to fifteen thousand built the railroad, "not a single letter, not a sole diary entry has been found." *West*, which originated when Rekdal was commissioned to write a poem commemorating the 150th anniversary of the transcontinental railroad, is an answer to this void. By weaving historical documents with her own work, Rekdal creates a space where a multitude of voices coexist, contradict, and reveal compounding repercussions.

The book is structured in two parts. The first, "West," is primarily poems interwoven with found materials: photographs, newspaper clippings, letters. Each poem has a corresponding section in part 2, "Notes Toward an Untranslated Century," an extended prose essay that annotates and elucidates the context of the poem it refers back to, while continuing and deepening critical and lyrical moments. "West" begins and ends with a poem "carved by an anonymous writer into the walls of the Angel Island Immigration Station" that is the heart and backbone of the book. The poem appears first as a transcription in Chinese and later as a loose translation by Rekdal. Following the passage of the Chinese Exclusion Act of 1882, Chinese detainees were held at Angel Island for as long as twenty-two months, and some who faced deportation committed suicide. This poem is an elegy responding to one such death:

> Sorrowful news indeed has passed to me.
> I mourn you: on what day will your wrapped body return?
> Unable to shut your eyes, to whom can you tell your story?
> Had you known, you never would have made this journey.
> A thousand ages now hold the sorrow of a thousand regrets.
> Missing home, you face in vain Home-Gazing Terrace,
> your ambitions, unfulfilled, buried under earth.
> Yet I know death can't turn your great heart to ashes.

Rekdal traces her lineage to Guangzhou, where many of the workers emigrated from. Yet she does not speak Chinese, and has created this translation of the poem based on literal meanings, as part of a consideration of her relationship to language and heritage that permeates the book.

Each word of the Angel Island translation is also a title of a poem in the book. In the Table of Contents, titles are presented with their corresponding Chinese characters, and the list of titles reads as yet another poem in translation. For instance, the final titles form the haunting phrase "Your" "Heroic" "Heart" "Dead" "Not Ash"—indicating that the entire book is a translation of the anonymous elegy, meant to fill in the gaps of what is known. So much is lost and left out of the story, Rekdal writes, including a partner poem to the Angel Island poem, which she does not publish: "Into this absence, I lean and angle my mirror."

West has a notably extensive companion website that features audio of Rekdal reading the poems, as well as multimedia arrangements of archival materials and other recordings. Each poem is linked to the corresponding title character in the Angel Island poem, which serves as a landing page. Rekdal writes of the website, "Visitors of 'West' can enter this poem either in the order of the characters or at random, thus producing their own translation of the poem by choosing how to enter it and reassemble its meaning online."

What Rekdal finds in the absence of history are voices. The poems "Able," "Should Know," and "Antiquity" use language from a

Chinese/English phrasebook to tell the story of an imagined Chinese immigrant seeking domestic work in the United States. "Able" begins optimistically:

> My name is Ah Quong.
> I was cook for Mrs. Black on Tenth street for three years.
> I can bring you good references.

Using short declarative sentences with deceptively simple syntax, mimicking the introductory language from the phrasebook, Rekdal builds a heartbreaking and nuanced story of the struggle this individual—and others in their position—likely faced. The poems form a progression, spaced throughout the book, and by the second, "Should Know," the worker's situation has become grim:

> He claimed my mine.
> He squatted on my lot.
> He took it from me by violence.
> I understand every word you say.

Here, a sense of futility and anger bubbles out through the declarative sentences, the simple and clear grievance. The corresponding note for "Should Know" is simply a list of places in the West where Chinese residents "were lynched, massacred, murdered, or attacked on account of their race during the 19th century."

In "Antiquity," the third poem in the progression, the narrative has progressed to hopelessness at the violence:

> The news now is very old.
> He was murdered by a thief.
> He was choked to death with a lasso.
> He committed suicide.

The story expands from the specific to the universal through these three different deaths. Now the simple declarative sentences are deflated, quiet, filled with grief as well as despair at the ubiquity of the events in each statement.

"Who is it, really, who made the writing of this book possible?" Rekdal asks. She inhabits voices of other peoples marginalized during this period: the impoverished Irish immigrants—"like the Chinese, almost universally despised"—who faced starvation and cholera; the

Cheyenne, Arapho, Ute, Lakota, and other Indigenous peoples whose lands and lives were invaded by the transcontinental railroad; the Black train porter and labor leader, who struggled for respect and justice; the orphans who were trafficked westward from the East Coast into servitude. Through persona poems, Rekdal inhabits the voices of the powerful as well—a California Supreme Court Justice-turned-lawyer for Central Pacific; Brigham Young; writers and reporters of the time; white labor leaders; and the founder of Stanford (who advocated for anti-Chinese immigration legislation). All of these voices, reflecting a multifaceted moment in history, contribute to this story.

Rekdal trains her mirror on more venerated figures, too—in "Sorrowful News," Lincoln's funeral procession (his coffin was transported across the country by train) is reported on by telegraph,

> across telegraph poles tall as the gallows
> from which the president
> ordered 38 Dakota hanged.

In the accompanying note, Rekdal considers her family's lineage, comparing her grandfather's open-casket funeral with the grandeur of Lincoln's and the anonymity of the murdered Dakota: "What do we seek from death's display?" Ten thousand people came to see Lincoln's funeral tour, but "the bodies of the Dakota Sioux … hung for less than an hour before being dumped in a mass grave." The poem brings a layered sense of irony in this re-reading of history, asking a question that seems to live in the space between the Civil War and today: "Can you believe still in the promise of this union?"

The contrapuntal poem "Sad" uses language from campaign speeches of presidents Andrew Johnson and Donald Trump side by side, such that it's impossible not to read them as in direct dialogue with one another: "There are a good many people," states Johnson, "but this is a country for white men." Notably, Johnson was labeled a "vulgar, drunken demagogue who was disgracing the presidency" by reporters at the time, and like Trump was impeached for abuse of power and obstruction of Congress. On the Trump side, we get familiar inflammatory excerpts like "They're bringing drugs, they're bringing crimes. Sad!" as well as "that Chinese virus I call it." In this poem we can see the white supremacy braided throughout the nation's psyche and language over centuries. In the note, Rekdal enumerates a spate of hate crimes and anti-Asian violence following 2020 and asks, "When a man stands behind a platform calling another man a virus, what is the reach of this language?"

Above all, *West* is a project of discovery and memory. Rekdal seeks a more complete history—of the nation, of the railroad, of individuals whose stories have been lost, of her family—and makes this history visible. She breaks open the idea of what a nation might be. "The railroad as metaphor insists we belong to one another through the work of nation-building," she writes, "while the poem insists we belong to one another because we are human." It is that belief that we will need to carry forward into the evolving story of America.

MARK WALSH

Imagine That By Judith O'Connell Hoyer
FutureCycle Press 2023

There's a moment in the sixth season of _The Great British Baking Show_ where judges Paul Hollywood and Prue Leith get a breakdown of contestant Kim-Joy's "signature bake." Kim-Joy ticks off seasonings, fruits, and flavors for the smiling judges: "I'm sure it will all be subtle," Leith remarks. I thought of this line as I read Judith O'Connell Hoyer's new book, _Imagine That_. The collection is broad in scope, but images and connections unfold with considerable subtlety. There is much to chew on here, and much in the aftertaste to consider.

Imagine That can feel like a sweeping family saga, shifting from various initiations into the adult world to quiet observations of death and loss, and again to poems that reveal the depth of love and reaffirm the power of seeing the world. Through poems of delicacy and grace, we see a life continually opening out.

Preservation is on Hoyer's mind; many of the poems reach out to memory and personal history in an attempt hold the hard-to-capture moments that define family, home, and place. All of this is woven together in "Scent of Lilacs":

> He is gone
> yet every May
> the scent is back
> to second grade,
> to those blossoms
> shaped like lungs,
> to Miss Gilligan
> leaning over my desk
> with her sharp pencil
> teaching me
> how to subtract.

Memory as scent, lilacs as lungs. These are apt connections, but the gesture and image of the final lines is less expected—the sharp pencil "subtracts" with clinical precision. You need to be made aware of loss before you really feel it.

Poems like "Wonder" and "Evening Bag" explore the dangerous adult world that borders childhood, presenting an innocent speaker who suspects that there are not-so-innocent things just beyond the boundaries of the family home. "Wonder" gives us a glimpse of that bigger, unsettling world

> [...] where only kids went,
> two men in singlets and boxer shorts
> dashed, one behind the other into the woods.
> Nothing I had ever seen.
> Spare saplings, they strung the undergrowth
> with switches stripped from hanging branches
> frantic to escape the yelp of hounds.

Adulthood brings this passage into high definition; we know these men are either dangerous or in danger (or both) and might guess at the background situation out of experience with the menaces in the larger world. Still, the moment stuns us, like the speaker, with its foreboding. In a similar manner, "Evening Bag" hints at adult complexities beneath the surface of a high school prom:

> There's a hole in the lining the size of a white lie
> my grandmother might have told my mother
> about what happened that night.
> It's been kept since the prom when it hung
> by its chain on the back of her chair
> as she waltzed onto the dance floor.

Here, the "white lie" and the evening bag's chain reveal more than a full story ever could.

The gentleness of these poems coaxes the reader—you linger in them as you do in old box of letters in your grandparents' attic: there's a whole world of small things there that might provide big answers. With the speaker's growth and experience, *Imagine That* expands its horizon from what's observed at home to what's observed abroad. In the poem "Anticipation" the home space not only includes family heirlooms, but a closet of clothes that serves as the tripwire for memories of Paris:

Our mouths meet at a kitchen table in Nantes.
The four of us conjure an amazing meal of oysters, octopus,
mackerel, champagne, and old, hard, salty orange cheese.
Bien sûr! Another bottle on the table.
Pears. *Merci.* Camembert. *Merci.*
Sancerre. *Merci. Oui,* the pretty glasses.

This catalog-menu carries echoes of Rexroth's dinner at Le Mistral, recalled in *The Dragon and The Unicorn*, that makes you want to pack a bag. O'Connell Hoyer may get you checking air fares. But more than mere travelogs, poems like "Anticipation" balance the tones of *Imagine That*, mixing the heavy with the light, offsetting darker notes with brighter ones. Playful poems add to the variety of moods in *Imagine That*, and they can become expansive. "Inheritance" focuses on a moment of good news after a health scare:

I'm reading *Great Expectations* for a second time.
Yesterday I bought two pairs of heels instead of one.
I'm not sending Christmas cards this year.
Blessings in disguise.

A clean bill of health resonates beyond the speaker's personal experience; we feel a connection stronger than we might have expected. Aren't we all there right now? After Covid, we can easily appreciate the gift of time, the glorious second chance that allows us to reset and take our lives in a new direction. We can buy shoes for different occasions— there are social occasions again!—even if they are superfluous. At a time like this, who doesn't want to reimagine their great expectations?

CONTRIBUTORS' NOTES

KATHLEEN AGUERO's latest book is *World Happiness Index*. Her other collections include *After That, Investigations: The Mystery of the Girl Sleuth, Daughter Of, The Real Weather*, and *Thirsty Day*. She has also co-edited three volumes of multicultural literature for the University of Georgia Press. She teaches in the Solstice low-residency M.F.A. program and in Changing Lives through Literature, an alternative sentencing program.

MARIA LUISA ARROYO CRUZADO was born in Manatí, PR and raised in the North End of Springfield, MA. She writes poems and essays that reflect the cultures and languages dynamically intersecting in her life experiences and imagination: American English, Puerto Rican Spanish, German, and Farsi, spoken in Iran. Her collections include *Gathering Words: Recogiendo palabras* (2008); two chapbooks *Flight* (2016), and *Destierro Means More than Exile* (2018); and her photo poem chapbook *Landscapes* (2023).

DEVON BALWIT walks in all weather. Her most recent collections are *We Are Procession, Seismograph* [Nixes Mate Books, 2017], *Dog-Walking in the Shadow of Pyongyang* [Nixes Mate Books, 2021] and *Spirit Spout* [Nixes Mate Books, 2023].

BRIAN MICHAEL BARBEITO is a Canadian poet, writer, and photographer. Recent work appears at *The Notre Dame Review*.

JENNIFER BARBER's four poetry collections are *The Sliding Boat Our Bodies Made* (The Word Works, 2022), *Works on Paper* (The Word Works, 2016), *Given Away* (Kore Press, 2012), and *Rigging the Wind* (Kore Press, 2003). She co-edited, with Jessica Greenbaum and Fred Marchant, the anthology *Tree Lines: 21st Century American Poems* (Grayson Books, 2022).

CYNTHIA BARGAR is Associate Poetry editor at *Pangyrus*. Her poems have appeared in many journals including *Nixes Mate, SWWIM Every Day, Driftwood Press, Rogue Agent, Book of Matches, LUMINA* and in the book, *Our Provincetown: Intimate Portraits* by Barbara E. Cohen (Provincetown Arts Press, 2021). Her poetry collection, *Sleeping in the Dead Girl's Room*, came out from *Lily Poetry Review Books* in January, 2022, and received 2023 Poetry Honors from the Massachusetts Society for the Book. Cynthia lives with her partner, cartoonist Nick Thorkelson, in Provincetown, Massachusetts.

JEANNE MARIE BEAUMONT is the author of four books of poetry: *Letters from Limbo, Burning of the Three Fires, Curious Conduct*, and *Placebo Effects*, and is co-editor of *The Poets' Grimm* anthology. Her play, *Asylum Song*, premiered at HERE Arts Theater in New York in 2019. Recent poems have appeared or are forthcoming in *Allium, Barrow Street, Cave Wall, Image, Southern Poetry Review, The Manhattan Review*, and *Verse Daily*. Her website is www.jeannemariebeaumont.com

LAURE-ANNE BOSSELAAR is the award-winning author of five poetry collections. Her next book: *Lately, New & Selected*, will come out in November 2023. The editor of five anthologies, she is the recipient of a Pushcart Prize and of the James Dickey Poetry Prize. She is Poet-at-Large at the Solstice Low Residency MFA program at Lasell University, and served as Santa Barbara's Poet Laureate from 2019 to 2021.

BARBARA SIEGEL CARLSON's third book of poems *What Drifted Here* was published by Cherry Grove Collections in 2023. Her previous books are *Once in Every Language* (Kelsay Books 2017) and *Fire Road* (Dream Horse Press 2013). A chapbook *Between the Hours* was published in 2022. Her poetry and translations have appeared in *The Cortland Review, Mid-American Review, American Journal of Poetry, Salamander, Ezra,* and *Avatar Review* among others. Carlson is Poetry in Translation Editor of *Solstice*.

LINDA CARNEY-GOODRICH is a writer and teacher whose work has appeared in *Nixes Mate, Anti-Heroin Chic, Muddy River, Literary Mama, Gyroscope, City of Notions: Anthology of Contemporary Boston Poems,* and forthcoming in *The MacGuffin*. Her poems have been displayed at Boston City Hall through the Mayor's Poetry Program. She is the Poetry Coordinator for the Menino Arts Center, and her first collection of poetry is forthcoming in 2024 from *Nixes Mate Books*.

MICHAEL J CARTER is a poet and psychotherapist who lives in Vermont. A graduate of Sarah Lawrence College he holds an MFA from Vermont College and an MSW from Smith. Poems of his have appeared in such journals as *Boulevard, Ploughshares, Mom Egg Review,* and *Western Humanities Review* among many others.

EILEEN CLEARY is the author of *Child ward of the Commonwealth* (2019), and *2 a.m. with Keats* (Nixes Mate, 2021). In addition, she co-edited the anthology *Voices Amidst the Virus*, the featured text at the 2021 Michigan State University Filmetry Festival and founded and is EIC of Lily Poetry review Books and *Lily Poetry Review*. Recent work is included in *Tree Lines: 21st Century American Poetry* just out through Grayson Books.

QUINTIN COLLINS (he/him) is a writer, assistant director of the Solstice MFA in Creative Writing Program, and a poetry editor for *Salamander*. He is the author of *The Dandelion Speaks of Survival* and *Claim Tickets for Stolen People*, selected by Marcus Jackson as winner of *The Journal*'s 2020 Charles B. Wheeler Prize. Quintin's other awards and accolades include a Pushcart Prize, the 2019 Atlantis Award from the Poet's Billow, and Best of the Net nominations.

WYN COOPER has published five books of poems, including, most recently, *Mars Poetica*. His poems have appeared in *The New Yorker, The Paris Review*, and *Poetry*, as well as in 25 anthologies of contemporary poetry. His poems have also been turned into songs by Sheryl Crow, David Broza, and Madison Smartt Bell. He lives in Vermont and works as a freelance editor. Concord Free Press published his first novel, *Way Out West*, in 2022.

STEVEN CRAMER's seventh poetry collection, *Departures from Rilke*, will be published by Arrowsmith Press in fall 2023. His previous books include *Listen* (MadHat Press); *Clangings* (Sarabande Books); and *Goodbye to the Orchard* (Sarabande), winner of the Sheila Motton Prize from the New England Poetry Club and a Massachusetts Honor Book. Recipient of fellowships from the Massachusetts Cultural Council and the National Endowment for the Arts, he founded and teaches in Lesley University's MFA Program in Creative Writing.

ALEXIS DAVID is a poet and fiction writer who holds a BA from Hobart and William Smith Colleges, an MS Ed from Canisius College, and an MFA from New England College. *Dancing Girl Press* published her chapbook *The Names of Animals I Have Loved*. Additionally, she has placed reviews of poetry for *Tupelo Quarterly, North of Oxford, Compulsive Reader* and *The Masters Review*. Links to her other published work can be found here: https://alexisldavid.wixsite.com/alexis.

WENDY DREXLER is a recipient of a 2022 artist fellowship from the Massachusetts Cultural Council. Her fourth collection, *Notes from the Column of Memory,* was published in September 2022 by *Terrapin Books*. Her poems have appeared in *Barrow Street, J Journal, Nimrod, Pangyrus, Prairie Schooner,* and *The Threepenny Review,* among others. She's been the poet in residence at New Mission High School in Hyde Park, MA, since 2018, and is programming co-chair for the New England Poetry Club.

KATHLEEN FRANK is a Santa Fe artist who paints the Western landscape in vibrant hues, capturing light and pattern in complex terrains. Career highlights include numerous museum and gallery exhibitions; High Desert Museum Curator's Choice Award; Art in Embassies/U.S. State Department selection - Kuala Lumpur, Malaysia; work in permanent collections; and features in numerous fine art publications.

JENNIFER FRANKLIN is the author of three full-length poetry collections, most recently, *If Some God Shakes Your House* (Four Way Books, March 2023). She is the recipient of a 2021 NYFA/City Artist Corps grant for poetry and a 2021 Café Royal Cultural Foundation Literature Award. She teaches craft workshops in Manhattanville's MFA program and manuscript revision at the Hudson Valley Writers Center, where she serves as Program Director. Visit her at jenniferfranklinpoet.com.

ROBBIE GAMBLE (he/him) is the author of *A Can of Pinto Beans* (Lily Poetry Review Press, 2022). His poems have appeared or are forthcoming in *Post Road, RHINO, Salamander, The Sun,* and *Whale Road Review.* He worked for many years as a nurse practitioner caring for people caught in homelessness, and he now divides his time between Boston and Vermont.

HANANYA GOODMAN is an asemic writer living in Ashdod, Israel. He has scripted over 20,000 unique asemic characters for his personal language. He is Director of Libraries at an engineering college, edited Between Jerusalem and Benares: Comparative Studies in Judaism and Hinduism, and written on kabbalah, geomancy and Einstein. His artwork can be seen at: https://www.facebook.com/hananya.goodman/ or https://www.instagram.com/hananyasart/

SONIA GREENFIELD (she/they) is the author of two recent collections of poetry, *All Possible Histories* (Riot in Your Throat, December 2022) and *Helen of Troy is High AF* (Harbor Editions, January 2023). She is the author of *Letdown* (White Pine Press, 2020), *American Parable* (Autumn House, 2018) and *Boy with a Halo at the Farmer's Market* (Codhill Press, 2015). Her work has appeared in the 2018 and 2010 *Best American Poetry, Southern Review, Willow Springs* and elsewhere. She lives with her family in Minneapolis where she teaches at Normandale College, edits the *Rise Up Review,* and advocates for both neurodiversity and the decentering of the cis/het white hegemony. More at soniagreenfield.com.

RYAN HARPER is the author of *My Beloved Had a Vineyard,* winner of the 2017 Prize Americana in poetry (Poetry Press of Press Americana, 2018). Some of his recent poems and essays have appeared in *Paperbark, Meniscus, Faux moir, Kithe, Consequence, Fatal Flaw, Cimarron Review,* and elsewhere. A resident of New York City, Ryan is the creative arts editor of *American Religion* Journal.

JANE POIRIER HART holds an MFA in Writing from Vermont College of Fine Arts and was a Poetry Fellow at the Writers' Room of Boston. Her work has appeared in print and online journals, including *Los Angeles Review, The Southern Poetry Review, The Worcester Review, The Ocean State Review, The Plath Poetry Project, Mason Street Review, and MER Vox Folio,* among others. She was a finalist for the Elyse Wolf Prize.

AMANDA HARTZELL is the author of two poetry books, *The Heart Never Pretends to Be a Beautiful Muscle* (Finishing Line Press) and *Glowing Animals* (Game Over Books). Her work was nominated for the Pushcart Prize and Best of the Net and appears in *Breakwater Review, Carve Magazine, New Letters,* and others. She holds an MFA from Emerson College in Boston. She lives and writes in Seattle with her husband, son, daughter, and their dog.

KRISTEN HEWITT has an MFA in poetry from Warren Wilson College. Her work has been published in *Orion*, Terrain.org, *LEON Literary Review*, *Whitefish Review*, *Jabberwock*, and *Kestrel*, and has been nominated for the Pushcart Prize. She was previously a Stone Court Writer-in-Residence. She's been an editor at *Orion* and the *Maine Review*, and currently edits nonfiction, comics, and children's books for PA Press. She lives in the Berkshires in western Massachusetts.

KAREN HILDEBRAND is the author of *Crossing Pleasure Avenue* (Indolent Books, 2018). She reviews dance for *Fjord Review* and *The Brooklyn Rail*, and recent poems have appeared in *Defunct, LEON, Maintenant, No Dear, Pigeon Pages, Poetry Bay, Quarter After Eight, Scoundrel Time, Slipstream, South Florida Poetry Journal*, and *Trailer Park Quarterly*. She holds an MFA from the Program for Writers at Warren Wilson College. Originally from Colorado, she lives in Brooklyn.

MARY HUTCHINS HARRIS's work has appeared in *Tar River Poetry, Kakalak, Main Street Rag, Poemeleon, Priene's Fountain, The Rumpus: ENOUGH, Ekphrastic Review, Spillway, Feminine Rising: Voices of Power and Invisibility*, as well as in other print and on-line publications. She is an Interdisciplinary Studies Adjunct professor in the Lesley University, Cambridge, MA Low-Residency MFA program and on the faculty of the YMCA Downtown Writer's Center in Syracuse, NY.

REUBEN JACKSON is the Archivist with the University of the District of Columbia's Felix E. Grant Jazz Archives. He is also co-host of WPFW's The Sound of Surprise. His poems have been included in over 50 anthologies, and in two volumes of poetry: *fingering the keys* (1991- Gut Punch Press)- and *Scattered Clouds*. (2019 - Alan Squire Publishers). He lives in Washington, D.C.

JULES JACOB is the author of *Kingdom of Glass & Seed* (Lily Poetry Review Books, 2023), *The Glass Sponge* (FLP), and the illustrated chapbook, *Rappaccini's Garden* (White Stag Press, December 2023), co-authored with Sonja Johanson. Jules is the recipient of a fellowship from the Virginia Center for the Creative Arts in France with poems featured or forthcoming in *Plume, Rust + Moth, Lily Poetry Review, The Fourth River, The Westchester Review* and elsewhere. Visit julesjacob.com.

CHRISTINE JONES lives in Orleans, MA and is the author of *Now Calls Me Daughter* (Nixes Mate Review, 2022) and *Girl Without a Shirt* (Finishing Line Press, 2020), also co-editor of the anthology, *Voices Amidst the Virus: Poets Respond to the Pandemic* (Lily Poetry Review Books, 2020). She is the founder/editor-in-chief of *Poems2go* and associate editor of *Lily Poetry Review*. Her poetry can be found in numerous journals and anthologies in print and online.

MICHAEL JONES' poetry appears in journals such as *Atlanta Review, Beloit Poetry Journal, Salamander,* and *Sugar House,* and in a chapbook, *Moved* (Kattywompus, 2016). A schoolteacher since 1990, he performed as a violinist with the Jupiter Chamber Players from 1998-2020.

GORDON KIPPOLA spent thirty-one years as a U.S. Army musician, earned an MFA in Creative Writing at the University of Tampa, and now calls Bremerton, Washington home. His poetry has appeared in *Rattle, Post Road Magazine, District Lit, The Main Street Rag, Southeast Missouri State University Press,* and other splendid publications.

ELIZABETH KUELBS writes at the edge of a Los Angeles canyon. Her work appears or is forthcoming in *Scientific American, Rust & Moth, Claw & Blossom, Poets Reading the News, HOOT Review, The Ekphrastic Review,* and other publications. A Pushcart Prize nominee, she holds an MFA from Vermont College of Fine Arts, and her chapbooks include *Little Victory* and *How to Clean Your Eyes.* Visit her online at https://elizabethkuelbs.com/.

ASHLEY KUNSA's recent poetry appears in *Massachusetts Review, Barrow Street, Cream City Review,* and *Southern Humanities Review.* Originally from Pittsburgh, she is currently assistant professor of creative writing at Rocky Mountain College in Billings, MT, where she lives with her husband and two children. You can find her online at www.ashleykunsa.com.

K.T. LANDON is the author of *Orange, Dreaming* (Five Oaks Press, 2017) and received her MFA from Vermont College of Fine Arts. Her work has appeared in *The Southern Review, The Sun, New Ohio Review, Nimrod, North American Review,* and *Best New Poets.* She is a reader for *Lily Poetry Review.*

MOIRA MAGNESON calls the Sierra foothills home and taught English for many years at Sacramento City College. Prior to teaching, she worked as a river guide throughout the West. Her poems have appeared in a variety of journals, including most recently the *New Verse News, Voices 2022, Persimmon Tree, Plainsongs,* and *California Fire and Water — A Climate Crisis Anthology.* Her full-length collection of poems, *In the Eye of the Elephant,* will be published by Sixteen Rivers Press in 2025.

JENNIFER MARTELLI is the author of *The Queen of Queens* (named a "Must Read by the Massachusetts Center for the Book), and *My Tarantella,* also named a "Must Read" by the Massachusetts Center for the Book, and awarded finalist for the Housatonic Book Award. Her work has appeared in *Poetry,* The Academy of American Poets *Poem-a-Day, Jet Fuel Review, Folio, Thrush,* and elsewhere. Jennifer Martelli has twice received grants for poetry from the Massachusetts Cultural Council. She is co-poetry editor for *Mom Egg Review.*

GRACE MASSEY is a retired editor and curriculum designer who spends as much time as possible socializing feral cats, taking ballet and Baroque dance classes, and working in her garden. Her poem "The Sightings of Birds" has been nominated for *Best of the Net Anthology*, 2023. Her poems have been published in *Thimble, Soul-Lit, Quartet, Frost Meadow Review, The Tiger Moth Review, Feral*, and elsewhere. She has degrees in English from Smith College and Boston University and lives in Newton, Massachusetts.

LIBBY MAXEY is a senior editor at *Literary Mama* and a winner of the 2021 Princemere Poetry Prize. Her work has appeared in *Emrys, The Maynard, Crannóg Magazine* and elsewhere, and her chapbook, *Kairos* (2019), won *Finishing Line Press's* New Women's Voices contest. Her nonliterary activities include singing classical repertoire and mothering sons. She lives with her family in Western Massachusetts.

SRI SOEKARMOEN MCCARTHY-OETJOEN is an Asian American artist who was born and spent her childhood in West Java, Indonesia. Mostly self-taught, her journey as an artist began in 2015. To her friends and family, McCarthy is called by her nickname, OETJOEN. Her cheerful personality and multicultural background are reflected throughout her work. Her approach to making art is "Let's throw colors and see what happens." Many of her works can be found at galleries in West Michigan and Minneapolis, Minnesota, and Allartwork.com. She resides in West Michigan with her husband and a black cat named Minmei.

ASKOLD MELNYCZUK has published four novels and a book of stories, *The Man Who Would Not Bow*. He's edited a book on Derek Walcott as well as an anthology of contemporary Ukrainian poetry and fiction. He's the publisher of Arrowsmith Press.

ELIZABETH MERCURIO (she/her) is the author of the chapbooks *Doll* and Words in a Night Jar. She is an Assistant Editor at *Lily Poetry Review*. She earned an MFA in poetry from The Solstice Low-Residency Program. Her work has appeared in *Ample Remains, The Wild Word, Thimble Magazine, Vox Populi*, and elsewhere. She was recently named a finalist in the Cordella Press Gwendolyn Brooks Poetry Prize and the Two Sylvias Press Wilder Poetry Prize. You can find her at: https://www.elizabethmercurio.com/

SUZANNE MERCURY's publications include *Sassafracas* (Xerolage 69), a collection of photographs of her glass poems (2018, Xexoxial Editions) and *Hand to Earth* (2019, Portable Press at Yo-Yo Labs). Her poetry has also appeared in a variety of publications including *SpoKe, Truck, Summer Stock, Bombay Gin, Sonora Review, Arts & Letters, Lily Poetry Review*, and *Hayden's Ferry Review*, as well as in the anthologies *Let the Bucket Down* and *The Wisdoms of the Universes in a Single String of Letters*. Her book *Hive* is forthcoming from *Lily Poetry Review Books*.

GLORIA MINDOCK is editor of Červená Barva Press. She is the author
of 6 poetry collections and 3 chapbooks. Her poems have been published
and translated into eleven languages. Her recent book, *Ash* (Glass Lyre Press,
2021) has received 7 book awards and was translated into Serbian by Milutin
Durickovic and published in Belgrade in 2022. Gloria was the Poet Laureate in
Somerville, MA in 2017 & 2018. www.gloriamindock.com

THERESA MONTEIRO is a former teacher and holds an MFA from
the University of New Hampshire. She has had poems published in various
magazines and journals *including The American Journal of Poetry, On the Seawall,
River Heron Review, Presence, Cutleaf Journal,* and *The Banyan Review*. Her work
has been nominated for a Pushcart Prize and her first full-length manuscript,
Under This Roof, is forthcoming from Fernwood Press. Theresa lives in New
Hampshire with her husband and children.

STEPHEN NELSON's latest book of visual poetry is called *Toys for
Telepaths* (Redfox Press). He has exhibited visual poetry and published prose
and poetry internationally for a number of years. He lives by the Cadzow Burn
in Central Scotland. See his asemic writing on Instagram @afterlights70.

CATHY MCARTHUR PALERMO's poetry was recently a semifi-
nalist for the *Crab Creek Review* Poetry Prize and has also appeared in *Lily Poetry
Review, The Rumpus, Jacket, Juked, Barrow Street, Gargoyle, Valparaiso Poetry Review,*
and *The Bellevue Literary Review* among others. Her flash fiction was shortlisted
in *The New Flash Fiction Review* and has appeared in *Peatsmoke.* She has taught
creative writing at several colleges in The City University of New York and for
The Lighthouse Guild.

KYLE POTVIN's debut full-length poetry collection is *Loosen*
(Hobblebush Books, 2021). Her chapbook, *Sound Travels on Water,* won the
Jean Pedrick Chapbook Award. Her poems have appeared in *Bellevue Literary
Review, Tar River Poetry, Lily Poetry Review, Ecotone, The New York Times,* and
others. She is a peer reviewer for *Whale Road Review.* Kyle lives on the Seacoast
of New Hampshire.

DANIEL PRITCHARD is a poet, translator, and essayist, as well as the
founding editor of *The Critical Flame* (criticalflame.org), an online journal of
literary criticism and nonfiction. His writing has appeared in *Sepia, Pangyrus,
The Wild Word, The Harvard Review Online, The Missouri Review,* and elsewhere.
Readers can find him at danielpritchard.net.

BETTE RIDGEWAY has exhibited globally for over four decades
with 80+ prestigious venues, including: Palais Royale, Paris and Embassy
of Madagascar. Awards include Top 60 Contemporary Masters and the
Leonardo DaVinci Prize. Mayo Clinic and Federal Reserve Bank top
Ridgeway's permanent collections. Books include *International Contemporary
Masters* and *100 Famous Contemporary Artists.*

STEVEN RIEL is the author of two full-length collections of poetry: *Edgemere* and *Fellow Odd Fellow*. His chapbook *Postcard from P-town* was published as runner-up for the inaugural Robin Becker Chapbook Prize. His poems have appeared in *The Minnesota Review* and *International Poetry Review*. He edits the Franco-American journal *Résonance*. Recipient of a Massachusetts Cultural Council grant, Riel was also named the 2005 Robert Fraser Distinguished Visiting Poet at Bucks County (PA) Community College.

MARYBETH RUA-LARSEN lives on the South Coast of Massachusetts. Her poems have appeared in *Magma, Orbis, Crannóg, Measure* and *American Arts Quarterly*, among others. She won the 2011 Over the Edge New Writer of the Year Competition in Poetry in Galway, Ireland; the 2016 Parent-Writer Fellowship in Poetry from the Martha's Vineyard Institute of Creative Writing; the 2017 Luso-American Fellowship for the DISQUIET International Literary Program in Lisbon, Portugal. She was a Hawthornden Fellow in Scotland in 2019, and in June 2022, she was chosen for inclusion in Marge Piercy's Summer Poetry Intensive Workshop in Wellfleet. Her chapbook *Nothing In-Between* is available from Barefoot Muse Press.

AMANDA RUSSELL (she/her) is an editor at *The Comstock Review* and a stay-at-home mom. Her poems are forthcoming or have appeared in *Hole in the Head re:View, EcoTheo Review, South Florida Poetry Journal,* and the anthology *mightier: poets for social justice*. To learn more about her or her chapbook, *Barren Years*, please visit https://poetrussell.wordpress.com/ or connect with her on Instagram: @poet_russell.

AMANDA SHAW graduated from the Warren Wilson MFA Program for Writers in January 2020. Since then, she has been a caretaker for her mother and working as an editor and teacher. She currently divides her time between New Hampshire and Washington, D.C. Her forthcoming manuscript, *It Will Have Been So Beautiful,* explores the search for a sense of place amid displacement, including the geographical and psychic displacements induced by climate change.

CATHERINE EATON SKINNER (Seattle/Santa Fe) illuminates the balance of opposites, reflecting mankind's attempts at connection. Skinner has an extensive global museum/gallery exhibition history, including Pie Projects, Las Cruces Museum: Branigan Cultural Center, and upcoming International Art Museum of America. 150+ publications have featured her work. Radius Books published her "monograph 108."

MAC STERN is a high school senior hailing from Northern California. He is a California State Summer School for the Arts alumnus for Creative Writing, as well as a 2023 National Young Arts Week Finalist in Scriptwriting. In his free time, he enjoys filmmaking, playing guitar, going to punk shows, and consuming queer media.

LINDA ANN STRANG's poetry collections are *Star Reverse* (Dryad Press, 2022) and *Wedding Underwear for Mermaids* (Honest Publishing, 2011). Her poetry and fiction have appeared in many journals, including *Portland Review, The Malahat Review, Hunger Mountain, Reflex Press*, and *Gone Lawn*. Linda is the co-founder and editor-in-chief of *Hotazel Review*. She lives in South Africa.

DANIEL B. SUMMERHILL has earned fellowships from Baldwin for the Arts and The Watering Hole. He is the inaugural Poet Laureate of Monterey County and has published two collections, *Divine, Divine, Divine* and *Mausoleum of Flowers*. His poems and essays appear in *The Academy of American Poets, Columbia Journal, Obsidian, The Wall Street Journal* and elsewhere. An Oakland native, Daniel lives in the Bay Area and is Professor of Poetry at Santa Clara University.

MARIA SURRICCHIO is originally from the UK and now lives near Boulder, Colorado. A life-long lover of poetry, she began writing in 2020 after a long marketing career. Pushcart nominated, her work has been published, and is forthcoming, in *Pirene's Fountain, The Comstock Review, Rust & Moth, The Café Review, I-70 Review*, and elsewhere. She has a BA in Modern Languages from Cambridge University and is an MFA candidate at Pacific University.

COLE SWENSEN is the author of 19 books of poetry, most recently, *And And And* (2022) and *Art in Time* (2021). A former Guggenheim Fellow, she's a recipient of the Iowa Poetry Prize, the SF State Poetry Center Book Award, the National Poetry Series, and the PEN USA Award in Translation and has been a finalist for the National Book Award. She divides her time between Paris and Providence RI, where she teaches at Brown.

KAREEM TAYYAR's most recent book, 'Keats in San Francisco & Other Poems,' was published in 2022 by *Lily Poetry Review Books*.

HEATHER TRESELER is the author of the forthcoming *Auguries & Divinations*, which received the 2023 May Sarton Book Prize from Bauhan Publishing, and *Parturition*, which received the international chapbook prize from the Munster Literature Centre in Ireland. Her poems appear in *Kenyon Review, Narrative, The Irish Times, Harvard Review*, and *The Iowa Review*, and have received the *Missouri Review*'s Editors' Prize and the W. B. Yeats Prize. She is professor of English at Worcester State University.

TERRY TROWBRIDGE is grateful to the Ontario Arts Council for his first writing grant, and the opportunities they enabled.

ANASTASIA VASSOS has been nominated for the Pushcart Prize, Best of the Net, and Best New Poets. She is the author of *Nike Adjusting Her Sandal* (Nixes Mate, 2021) and *Nostos* (Kelsay Books, 2023.) *Nostos* was named a finalist in Two Sylvias' and Headlight Review's Chapbook Contests. Her

poems appear in *Thrush, SWWIM, RHINO, Whale Road Review,* and elsewhere.
She speaks three languages, reads for *Lily Poetry Review,* and lives in Boston.

TOM VERSTEEG's poems have appeared in a variety of journals,
Mid-American Review, Birmingham Poetry Review, Bellingham Review, and *Camas*
among them.

CONNEMARA WADSWORTH's chapbook, *The Possibility of
Scorpions,* about the years her family lived in Iraq in the early 50's, won the
White Eagle Coffee Store Press 2009 Chapbook Contest. Her poems are
forthcoming or appeared in *Prairie Schooner, Solstice, Chautauqua, Bellevue Literary
Review,* and *Valparaiso.* Her poem, "Mediation on a Photo" was a winner of The
Griffin Museum of Photography's Once Upon a Time: Photos That Inspire
Tall Tales. She lives in Newton, Massachusetts.

MARK WALSH is an English professor at Massasoit Community College
in Brockton, MA, where he teaches literature and philosophy. He is a submis-
sions reader for The *Lily Poetry Review,* and his book reviews have appeared
in the *Lily Poetry Review* and *Solstice.* His poetry publications include *Beatnick
Cowboy, Lily Poetry Review, Wilderness House Literary Review* and *Abandoned Mine.*

ANTHONY WALTON is the author of *Mississippi: An American Journey,*
and the editor, with Michael S. Harper, of *The Vintage Anthology of African
American Poetry* and *Every Shut-Eye Ain't Asleep: African American Poetry Since
World War II.* His poems have appeared in *The New Yorker, Black Scholar, Oxford
American, Poetry Ireland Review, Ecotone, 32 Poems, Notre Dame Review, Alaska
Quarterly Review, Kenyon Review,* and *The Library of America: African American Poetry,*
among many other magazines, journals, and anthologies. The recipient of a
Whiting Award, he teaches at Bowdoin College.

PAMELA WAX, an ordained rabbi, is the author of *Walking the
Labyrinth* (Main Street Rag, 2022) and the chapbook, *Starter Mothers* (Finishing
Line Press 2023). Her poems have received a Best of the Net nomination
and awards from *Crosswinds, Paterson Literary Review, Poets' Billow, Oberon,* and
Robinson Jeffers Tor House. She has been published in journals includ-
ing *Barrow Street, Tupelo Quarterly, Mudfish, About Place Journal, Naugatuck River
Review, Pedestal, Split Rock Review,* and *Passengers Journal.*

SANDY WEISMAN is both poet and visual artist. Her poetry has been
included in two anthologies and several other journals, including *Salamander,
Spillway, Barrow Street, The Maine Review, Off the Coast,* and *Muddy River Poetry
Review.* Her artists books can be seen this fall at University of Southern Maine,
Portland, and the Michael Good Gallery, Rockport. Sandy is the owner of 26
Split Rock Cove, a privately-owned artist community of studios, artist living
space, and workshops overlooking Mussel Ridge Channel in S. Thomaston,
ME. www.26splitrockcove.com

ROBERT WITMER has lived in Tokyo, Japan, for the past 45 years, having served as a Professor of English at Sophia University until his retirement in 2022. His poems have appeared in many journals and anthologies. His second book, *Serendipity*, a collection of prose poetry pieces and haiku sequences, was published in March 2023. His first book of poems, *Finding a Way*, was published in 2016.

ELLEN JUNE WRIGHT consulted on guides for three PBS poetry series. Her work has been featured by *Verse Daily*, *Rappahannock Review*, *The Good Life Review*, *Passengers Journal*, *Scoundrel Times*, *Banyan Review* and others. She's a Cave Canem and Hurston/Wright alumna and a 2021 and 2022 Pushcart Prize nominee. Follow her @ EllenJuneWrites on Instagram and Twitter.

GEORGE YATCHISIN is the author of *Feast Days* (Flutter Press 2016) and *The First Night We Thought the World Would End* (Brandenburg Press 2019). His poems have been published in journals including *Antioch Review*, *Askew*, and *Zocalo Public Square*. He is co-editor of the anthology *Rare Feathers: Poems on Birds & Art* (Gunpowder Press 2015), and his poetry appears in anthologies including *Reel Verse: Poems About the Movies* (Everyman's Library 2019).

CYNTHIA YATCHMAN is a Seattle-based artist and art instructor. She works primarily on paintings, prints, and collages. She shows extensively in the Pacific Northwest. Past shows have included Seattle University, the Tacoma and Seattle Convention Centers, and the Pacific Science Center. Her art is housed in numerous public and private collections.

www.ingramcontent.com/pod-product-compliance
Lightning Source LLC
Chambersburg PA
CBHW051508050726
47594CB00010B/4019